More than skin deep

More than skin deep:
Developing anti-racist multicultural education in schools

IAN MASSEY

Hodder & Stoughton

LONDON SYDNEY AUCKLAND TORONTO

E0005111109001.

for Jan, Tom and Alex

British Library Cataloguing in Publication Data
Massey, Ian
 More than skin deep : developing anti-racist multicultural
 education in schools.
 1. Great Britain. Multicultural education
 I. Title
 370.115

ISBN 0 340 52348 4

First published 1991

Typeset by Litho Link Limited, Welshpool, Powys, Wales
Printed in Great Britain for the educational publishing division of
Hodder and Stoughton Ltd, Mill Road, Dunton Green, Sevenoaks, Kent
by St Edmundsbury Press Ltd.

Contents

Acknowledgements vi

Introduction 1

1 Multicultural Britain: the six phases of school and LEA response 8

2 Clarifying the concepts 31

3 The new right: one Flew in the cuckoo's nest? 54

4 Anti-racist multicultural education in the new ERA 73

5 Making and managing change 103

6 Theory into practice: the Frogmore experience 127

Appendix 157

Bibliography 161

Index 175

Acknowledgements

This book owes a considerable debt to the work and advice of many colleagues, both inside and outside Frogmore Community School, over the last few years.

In the pre–Swann days there were not many schools in all-white areas that had the foresight to address the issues of cultural diversity and racism. At Frogmore there were teachers who were concerned about the racism of many of our pupils. That was our starting point. Unlike other schools, where there was also concern, Frogmore had the support of the then Headteacher, Dick Moss, to begin looking at ways in which that issue could be addressed through the formation of a Working Party along with the active participation and support of the Deputy, David Rowbotham.

It was this group of people who guided Frogmore's developments, and I owe a special thanks to the wisdom and professionalism of Keith Hurst, Joan Elkins, Sheila Ogden, Diane Nicholson, Martin, Curtis, Keith Imerson, Danny Brown, Jane Stuttard, Renata Coxon, Derek Dowden, Sue Bowers and John Tucker. The support of other colleagues, outside of that group, has also been crucial during the years of staff development, especially the personal and professional commitment of those in PE and Creative Arts and Humanities. The willingness of those in Mathematics, Design, Languages, Science and Home Economics to develop, and to try different approaches and extend their professionalism in the interests of providing students with a broad non-racist educational experience, provides a loud rejoinder to a much maligned profession.

The present school management team, led by Paul Harwood, deserves mention for its continued support and encouragement, as do recent additions to the working group, such as Janet Harrod, Richard Smith, Mark Scott and Malcolm Floyd.

The school and I benefited considerably from the help of the Team for Racial Equality in Education which was at that time based at Bulmershe College in Reading. The expertise of Marina Foster, Shamira Dhramshi and Pauline Lyesight-Jones was both a resource and a catalyst in the developments at Frogmore.

I am also grateful to Bob Brownhill of Surrey University and Viv Edwards of Birkbeck College for their advice and constructive comments on certain parts of this book.

I must also thank Alec Fyfe, Inspector for Intercultural Education in Hampshire, and Alec Roberts, Deputy Head at Park Community School, Havant, for their continued support and advice in this work, encouraging developments like those outlined in this book to take place in other institutions.

The Publishers would like to thank the following for permission to reproduce material in this volume:

Berkshire LEA for the extract from *Education for Racial Equality*, Policy Paper 1 (1983); Croom Helm Ltd for the extract from Verma and Bagley (eds) *Race Relations and Cultural Differences: Some Ideas on Racial Frame of Reference*; Falmer Press Ltd for the extract from 'Ideologies and Multicultural Education' from M. Craft (ed.) *Education and Cultural Pluralism*; Hampshire LEA for the extract from their literature; Harper and Row Ltd for the extract from *Ethnic Minorities in Education* by R. Jeffcoate (1984); HMSO for the extracts from *DES Circular*, May 1989, *From Policy to Practice, English 5–16, The Swann Report, Design and Technology for Ages 5–16* and *The Education Reform Act 1988*; Alfred A. Knopf Inc for the extract from *The Autobiography of an Ex-coloured Man* by James Weldon Johnson, copyright 1927 by Alfred A. Knopf Inc. and renewed 1955 by Carl Van Vechten; New Statesmen Society for the extract from 'I'm not National Front Myself but ...' by R. Cochrane and M. Billig from *New Society*, 17 May, 1984; Routledge and Kegan Paul for the extract from *Multicultural Education: Principles and Practice* by J. Lynch (1966); Trentham Books Ltd for the extracts from *Multicultural Teaching*, Vol. 13, No. 6, 1988 and 'Anti-racist Education after the Act' by Richard Hatcher from *Multicultural Teaching*, Vol. 7, No. 3, 1989.

Every effort has been made to trace and acknowledge ownership of copyright. The publishers will be glad to make suitable arrangements with copyright holders whom it has not been possible to contact.

Introduction

The end of the Second World War left its legacy for decades in all European countries, Eastern and Western, taking many different political and social forms. The often enforced Stalinism of eastern Europe survived until the end of the 1980s, when it dramatically collapsed under the weight of popular demands for greater social democracy. This also unleashed violent nationalistic tendencies in many states and a resurgence of anti-Semitism: a reminder that it is not only amongst ex-colonial capitalist countries that prejudice and racism can manifest themselves at a personal and institutional level.

For Britain, part of its Second World War legacy was to be the dismantling of a once-extensive Empire and a reassessment of its world role. In common with that of other western European countries, Britain's post-war labour shortage and reconstruction was met in significant parts by the recruitment of labour from the colonies or ex-colonies. In Britain's case, this meant mainly from the islands of the West Indies, together with India, Pakistan, Bangladesh and Hong Kong. In addition, there were refugees from Europe and Asians from East Africa, with the consequence that Britain's post-war society took on an increasingly multicultural dimension.

Britain, of course, has had a long history of immigration and settlement, including Roman, Celtic, Huguenot, Irish and Jewish peoples. There has also been a long-established black population in many cities, such as London, Cardiff and Liverpool, dating from the days of Britain's involvement in the notoriously barbaric slave trade.

The migration pattern throughout the 1950s and 1960s simply brought existing patterns of immigration into sharper relief. A country which once had a quarter of the world as its colonial Empire, now had, in Rushdie's phrase, 'A new Empire within' (1982).

From this 'new Empire' since the end of the war have risen some successful professionals, business people, teachers, politicians and academics. However, all research shows (see Chapter 3) that levels of discrimination remained high during this period and that the vast majority of ethnic minorities remained disproportionately in lower socio-economic groups and under-achieved in the education system.

In addition to levels of discrimination, it is estimated that since the war 70 people, including women and children, have been killed as the result of racist attacks and thousands have been injured (*Guardian*, 1989). This far exceeds the deaths and injuries in Britain directly attributable to another 'social disease', football hooliganism. (Even including the deaths of the 39 Italian supporters at the Heysel Stadium would not produce a comparable figure.)

The phenomenon of football violence began in the mid 1960s, and the 1970s and 1980s saw millions of pounds being spent on policing and stadium conversions. There were also millions of words expounded in the media, in Government reports, and in academic journals and books, especially after the 1985 Heysel Stadium tragedy. Along with Marxist and phenomenological explanations came the familiar cry for families and schools (especially comprehensives) to examine how they were preparing young people for the world and the values and behaviour they promoted and condoned. Sue Reid, in *The Mail on Sunday* (2 June, 1985) accused British schools of 'turning out an army of disaffected youths, illiterate and loutish' and the *Sunday Telegraph* claimed that 'It is the behaviour of the classroom which has now, in a magnified form invaded the football terraces.' Aubron Waugh in the *Spectator* (8 June, 1985) went on to develop this line of argument by calling for the 'dismantling of the entire secondary school system'. Writing in *The Times Educational Supplement* (7 June, 1985) Lawrence and Steed argued that not enough attention was being paid to the serious disruption going on in our schools, which was predisposing young people to this kind of violence, suggesting that the 'Failure of the family to socialise is compounded by the failure of the school as an agent of secondary socialisation.' It was seen as an appropriate concern for all schools.

The victims of racial violence, abuse and discrimination did not receive similar extensive and intensive attention (despite the passing of race relation laws) from the police or the media. The response of the education system to Britain's increasing diversity and the issues of racism, prejudice, discrimination and question of curriculum content are, of course, the subject of this book.

It was initially the efforts of black and Asian parents, teachers and educationalists that forced the education system to review its provision for ethnic minority children and their levels of achievement.

What became known as multicultural and anti-racist education in the 1970s and 1980s became associated in the minds of many Heads and teachers solely with the educational needs of ethnic minorities. The racial violence, abuse and discrimination practised by much of the white population was, unlike football hooliganism, not considered a relevant matter for all schools or society to address. For the mainly white school, not only was there 'no problem here' (to borrow Chris Gaine's phrase) because there were few ethnic minority pupils, but racism and discrimination were not seen as part of the pupil's frame of reference. Racism might exist, but certainly not here, in our school or among our pupils. It was always somewhere else, though attempts to locate it often proved it elusive.

The Swann Report (1985) did attempt to address the nature of the beast by its title, *Education for All*, and by stressing the need for all educational institutions to prepare all pupils for life in a multicultural society. This would involve examining resources for ethnocentric bias, combating racism and developing school policies. At last the 'all-white' dimension was recognised.

Unfortunately, the report did not offer practical guidance on how this could be implemented. (This book will suggest some possibilities.) Writing in 1986, Troyna and Williams acknowledged that anti-racist strategies developed in certain LEAs would not be entirely appropriate in all-white areas due to their different demographic, social and political context. One suggestion was that those involved in this kind of work in all-white areas could stress 'that educated citizens do not taunt visiting black footballers' (p. 123).

What lay behind this was the growth in the number of black people in certain sports, such as boxing, athletics and especially football during the 1970s and 1980s. Those who graduated to first-team football were soon made aware of British racism in no uncertain manner through the reaction of the crowd. All black footballers have tales of having bananas thrown at them, being spat at, the making of monkey noises, along with other loudly chanted racial taunts. The extent of this has not been fully realised by those who do not follow the game. One black player tells of how his manager substituted him in one First Division game to spare him the incessant racial abuse (Garth Crooks in conversation with Barry Norman, BBC, 2 January, 1980).

In the late 1980s Liverpool, Britain's top football club (which had alienated a lot of its potential black supporters and had not tapped the talent of a long-established black community) signed John Barnes, then Britain's most talented player, who also happened to be black. It was only then that the racist grafitti around the ground was tackled and senior individuals began to make public statements deploring such racist behaviour. His debut was marred by racial taunting from the opposing supporters, who included reference to the fact (rare today) that their team was all-white (see *Out of His Skin: the John Barnes Phenomenon* by Dave Hill, 1989, Faber & Faber).

This abuse was perpetuated and condoned by white citizens from more than one social class. It was heard on radio and television in homes throughout the land and, with one or two notable exceptions, went unremarked upon by reporters, commentators, managers, players, chairmen and the football authorities. Apart from the action on the field, the focus was always on supporters' violence or threat of violence. Great concern was voiced by pundits, virtually all white, about the image of a game so frequently associated with violence, yet rarely was concern expressed about the extent of displays of overt racism, nor was the role of the education system on this issue called into question as it so often was in discussion of hooliganism.

It was not until 1990 that the Taylor Inquiry into the deaths of 95 fans at Hillsborough, which was essentially concerned with crowd safety, made the additional suggestion that racial chanting be made an offence.

For black and Asian people, racism, overt and covert, was not something confined to match days: it had become a daily reality. Its manifestations included the job or flat that had 'just gone' and the need to seal up the letter box to prevent urine, excrement, or petrol and a match from dropping uninvited on to the mat.

It was in those areas of British cities where the daily reality for ethnic minorities was one of abuse and assault that some schools were forced into taking a more proactive role in the community through anti-racist initiatives. This was often organised in conjunction with parents and led to policy statements and curricular reviews. Those developments will be discussed in more detail later, but are acknowledged here as major catalysts for more wide spread changes involving a much larger number of pupils and students in mainly white areas.

This book aims to address specifically the promotion and

management of anti-racist multiculturalism in the all-white situation. The term 'all-white' or 'mainly white' should not be interpreted as ignoring the presence of children from various cultural or ethnic backgrounds in these schools. It is rather a crude shorthand description which recognises that such children often form a very small part of a school's intake. (The term 'black/Asian' is used for all those children and students of, mainly, former colonial immigrants, and is an even cruder shorthand description for a very diverse collection of people.) Consequently, the book does not deal directly with issues such as the levels of achievement and particular needs of black and Asian pupils, or the separate schools debate. This is not to devaluate their importance, as the levels of achievement of black and Asian pupils in the mainly white school are also a matter for consideration, along with their self-image.

An increase in the achievement level of ethnic minority pupils is, of course, to be welcomed, and there are signs that this is slowly emerging (see ILEA Exam Survey of 1989). However, a bag full of examination passes may be substantially devalued if the personal and institutional racism, intentional and unintentional, practised by the white population (including employers, politicians, administrators, police officers, journalists, social workers and football supporters) is allowed to remain unexamined and unchallenged. This book recognises that many of these positions will be filled by the pupils from the all-white classrooms and that all teachers have a professional responsibility to ensure that those children are adequately prepared for life in a multicultural society. In working towards that goal we also have to accept that racism and discrimination take many forms, overt and covert, intentional and unintentional. Also, many white British people who would never resort to racial violence or open abuse, continue to tell racist jokes, continue to discriminate, are uneasy with the growing diversity of Britain which manifests itself in daily life through shop and business ownership and through the symbols of success in car and house ownership. As Forsythe (1988) puts it:

> What, however, I have heard expressed over and over again in public houses, at gatherings in private houses, in humble cafés or well-accoutred restaurants is a heart-felt conviction among many whites that black and brown people should not have been brought here in the first place and they are not wanted as permanent fellow citizens. (p. 36)

This manifests itself in a variety of ways, from hostility to avoidance, from omission to paternalism. Consequently, we have to acknowledge that many of these negative attitudes towards cultural diversity are 'more than skin deep'. They have deep roots in our cultural history and education has played its part in this social process. An examination of the role of the school, its staff, its curriculum and ethos in the way it prepares pupils for life in a multicultural society is therefore of paramount importance. This is not an attempt to engender feelings of impotent guilt, but rather to begin to explore strategies which will enable us to confront the issues of racism, cultural diversity and good educational practice, both as individuals and as professional educators. Through this process we will hopefully avoid changes which are merely cosmetic and realise that the educational changes necessary will also have to be 'more than skin deep'.

The focus of this book is the particular context of the mainly white school and the managing of anti-racist multicultural change as we begin a new ERA of education. However, just as many of us learnt a great deal from the work undertaken in the multi-ethnic areas and schools of our larger cities, so, it is hoped that educationalists in those areas too, may they gain something from this book, especially in the management of change.

The book deals with the developments and responses of the education system since the increase in Britain's cultural diversity, from the end of the Second World War to the introduction of the National Curriculum. Many of the issues are indeed complex, especially as we enter a new ERA, and cannot be resolved in this book. What can be offered is a contribution to a continuing process, a reply to the recent wave of attacks on the growth of anti-racist multiculturalism and a case for the enrichment of pupils learning through the National Curriculum and the combating of racism in all schools. Practical suggestions are made of ways in which the change to an anti-racist multicultural curriculum can be managed, with indications of what the results may be in areas of the curriculum, school, ethos, pupil attitudes and parental awareness. This book is just one contribution in the continuing pursuit of racial and social justice.

The Pembertons looked up and saw Arnie coming, guiding Vivi by the hand. Grace Pemberton gasped and put her spoon back in the soup. Emily went pale. Mr Pemberton's mouth opened. All the Americans stared. Such a white, white girl and such a black, black boy coming across the dining room floor! The girl had a red mouth and grey eyes.

The Pembertons had been waiting for Arnie since four o'clock. Today a charming Indian mystic had come to tea with them, especially to see the young Negro student they had raised in America. The Pembertons were not pleased that Arnie had not been there.

'This is my friend,' Arnie said. 'I've brought her to dinner.'

Vivi smiled and held out her hand, but the Permbertons bowed in their stiffest fashion. Nobody noticed her hand.

'I'm sorry,' said Grace Pemberton,' but there's room for only four at our table'.

'Oh,' said Arnie. He hadn't thought they'd be rude. Polite and formal maybe, but not rude. 'Oh! Don't mind us then. Come on, Vivi.' His eyes were red as he led her away to a vacant table by the fountain. A waiter came and took their orders with the same deference he showed everyone else. The Pembertons looked but could not eat.

'Where ever did he get her?' whispered Emily in her thin New England voice, as her cheeks burned. 'Is she a woman from the streets?' The Pembertons couldn't imagine that so lovely a white girl would go out with a strange Negro unless she were a prostitute. They were terribly mortified. What would he do next?

Langston Hughes (1934)

1

Multicultural Britain: the six phases of school and LEA response

T he effects of the Second World War on European countries are still being felt today in a variety of ways. In some areas there are movements for reunification; in others movements for independence, with an accompanying nationalism which has been suppressed for over 40 years. For western European countries there has been a significant change in the make-up of their populations. This has been the result of migration from ex-colonies and poorer parts of Europe for political or economic reasons. In consequence, all western European countries have become more diverse, and this is especially true of the UK. There has had to be a close examination of the nature of the education system as a response to this change.

The end of the war presented Britain with labour problems which were caused by a mixture of genuine shortages and the rising expectations of Britain's indigenous working class. This led to labour shortages in specific jobs, especially those which involved little skill, unpleasant conditions, or anti-social hours. The solution was recruitment from the colonies and ex-colonies.

This pattern of migration can be seen in Britain's population figures which, in 1951 gave the non-white population as 0.25 per cent. By 1990 this had risen to 4.7 per cent (Labour Force Survey, 1990) Of this total, West Indians made up 0.9 per cent, Indians 1.4 per cent, Pakistanis 0.8 per cent, Bangledeshis 0.2 per cent, and mixed race making up 0.5 per cent. Figures such as these only touch on Britain's diversity as they do not reveal the diversity within these categories, of first and second generation people or language and religious differences. Figures are often published without reference to the migration of Australians, Irish and Europeans to Britain since the end of the Second World War. This is because immigration for many people, including the media and elected representatives of the people, came to be mean black immigration. As a result, it was this particular aspect of the post-war migration of people that led to social, legal, political and educational changes.

It is the response of the education system to Britain's current cultural diversity that is the subject of this work, especially as it relates to those areas of Britain which appear to remain untouched by the demographic and cultural changes brought about since the war. As Mary Fuller (1983) and Banks (1981) note, the education system seems to have passed through several phases, although, as Banks points out, 'the division between stages is blurred rather than sharp' (p. 134). Six stages can be identified, but there is, of course, considerable overlap.

1 LAISSEZ-FAIRE

The initial response to black and Asian immigration was, according to Rose (1969), inaction. The assumption was that everyone was equal before the law and, therefore, no special policies were necessary. Immigrants would learn to integrate by working and learning alongside whites. Immigrants were simply strangers who faced temporary difficulties which would be eased by assistance from voluntary agencies. Any tensions caused by their arrival would soon disappear as they were absorbed into an essentially tolerant society. In the early years of post-war immigration, most immigrants were male, and they saw their stay in Britain as temporary.

Kirp (1979) argues that there was no racially explicit policy at this time and that Government was hoping it would be helping non-whites by not favouring them explicitly.

However, Troyna and Williams (1986) argue that 'inaction or consistent decisions not to act also imply the existence of a policy' (p. 2). After all, decisions have to be taken not to act and that will be the consequence of an ideological position. The 'policy' of 'doing good by doing little' did not last long, as some of the assumptions on which it was based began to be questioned by the reactions of white people.

2 ASSIMILATION VIA LANGUAGE AND NUMBERS

In 1958 the first disturbances attributable to racial tension took place in Notting Hill. These led to calls from representatives of white communities at local and national level and for the Government to take more positive action.

The key to social cohesion was seen as assimilation of the immigrants and this would be assisted by greater control over the numbers allowed to enter the country. Under the 1948 Nationality Act, all peoples of the Commonwealth and colonies had full citizenship rights, including right of entry to Britain. In 1962 the first of several Immigration Acts was passed, which restricted the right of entry by drawing a line between those who were born in the United Kingdom and those who were born and resident in the independent countries of the Commonwealth or colonies. The latter would no longer possess automatic right of entry.

The educational response at this time was to offer infant and junior reception centres where children without English as a mother-tongue were given introductory courses. Lynch (1986a) argues that the developing policies towards Commonwealth immigrants contained a conviction of cultural superiority, subliminal prejudice and a secret commitment to racial discrimination through segregation in housing.

This obsession with numbers was reflected in DES *Circular 7/65* which gave LEAs permission for the dispersal or 'bussing' of immigrants. This would be done where the quota of immigrants exceeded 33 per cent of the school. The justification for such a policy was educational, based on language development and a furtherance of cultural assimilation. However, there were undoubtedly fears of a 'white backlash' as the document notes that:

> It will be helpful if the parents of non-immigrant children can see . . . that the progress of their own children is not being restricted by the undue preoccupation of the teaching staff with the linguistic and other difficulties of the immigrant children.

Although language development was used as the educational rationale for this policy, Milner (1983) has noticed that children were dispersed irrespective of whether they were new arrivals or not, without consultation with parents and 'irrespective of whether they had language difficulties or not' (p. 199). There is also no evidence on which to base the notion that white children would be held back by those children who had difficulties with English, or where the proportion of black and Asian children rose above 33 per cent (see Little, 1975). As white children were not bussed, the effect was racist and not many authorities implemented or continued to follow the policy. Pronouncements from Government departments and agencies stressed the importance of assimilation and cultural resocialisation.

The DES (1963) had stressed that the task of the education system was 'the successful assimilation of immigrant children' and the Commonwealth Immigrants Advisory Council report (1964) stated:

> If their parents were brought up in another culture or another tradition, children should be encouraged to respect it, but a national system [of education] cannot be expected to perpetuate the different values of immigrant groups (p. 7).

Assimilation was to be on the terms of the dominant groups in British society but presented in 'deracialised' terms. The policies and practices were legitimised in educational terms.

3 INTEGRATION THROUGH COMPENSATION

The initial policy response of the education system of language tuition was consolidated in 1966 through Section 11 funding, by which LEAs could claim back 50 per cent (later 75 per cent) of the cost of providing English as a second language tuition from the Home Office. It was also about this time that the notion of 'integration' became a popular concept, sometimes presented as a more sensitive development of assimilation. The key to successful integration was, as Barker (1981) wrote, 'linguistic integration as the precondition of social integration' (p. 75). Without this, cultural resocialisation was impossible. Accordingly, bilingualism was not considered an option for Commonwealth children. It was considered a disadvantage to learning, impeding social and intellectual development. This was the view of a DES report in 1971, which suggested that black students were at a disadvantage because the language heard at home was their native tongue or pidgin English. So, the report went on, 'against a background of this kind the best intentions of school can easily be nullified' (p. 65). Bilingualism was only to be encouraged, according to the Schools Council (1967), if it involved a language generally accepted as a foreign language within school. This, of course, restricted it to European languages such as French or Italian. Language tuition itself was mainly confined to Asian pupils and not extended to Afro-Caribbean children who were seen as speaking a deficient dialect of English which needed correction.

This view of the language and dialects of ethnic minorities reduced them to the status given to Bernstein's restricted speech code, supposedly spoken by and restricting the intellectual development of white working class pupils. Bernstein's work became closely associated with notions of cultural deprivation and programmes of compensatory education for working class pupils. However, as Flude (1974) pointed out, notions of cultural deprivation contained a normative concept of culture, which was white and middle class. All other cultures were valued according to how well they measured up to this ideal, and where they failed to, they were seen as deficient and inferior. Consequently, any problems ethnic minority children had were seen as the result of their cultural or linguistic deficiencies or family structure. Such a view enabled:

1 The school itself to remain unexamined in its role and method of educating pupils from ethnic minorities.

2 Policies and practices to be presented in a deracialised form, with fashionable educational criteria and concepts cited as legitimising agents to a racist posture.

3 Any lack or unwillingness to 'integrate' could be blamed on ethnic minorities themselves, as they had been given the opportunities to integrate into British culture.

The late 1960s saw a number of research studies which showed the extent of racial discrimination in Britain (e.g. Daniel, 1968), especially in the areas of employment and housing. Daniel described it as varying from 'the massive to the substantial' (p. 209). In 1969 a Select Committee on Race Relations and Immigration reported that, because of this situation and the attitudes of alienation and hostility seen in some black youths, Britain was sitting on a 'social time-bomb' which would go off if there were not steps to equalise the treatment and life experiences of ethnic minorities. Education was seen as having a vital part to play in convincing black and Asian youths that education was of value and in countering and preventing feelings of alienation and hostility.

4 MULTICULTURALISM: FROM COMPENSATION TO CULTURAL PLURALISM

The date usually acknowledged as being the beginning of this phase is 1966, when Roy Jenkins, then Home Secretary, introduced the notion of pluralism. This was not to be regarded as a flattening process of assimilation but as equal opportunity accompanied by cultural diversity in an atmosphere of mutual tolerance. However, practical educational activities based on this approach were a long time in developing. The report of the Select Committee on Race Relations and Immigration (1969) urged teaching about countries from which immigrants had come, including songs, art and costumes to 'help bring immigrant children into the life of the school' (p. 42). During the 1970s an approach to multictultural education developed which became known by many as the 3 S version – Saris, Samosas and Steel bands. This was characterised by Rushdie (1982) as 'teaching the kids a few bongo rhythms and how to tie a sari'. Caribbean Studies and Asian History were often additional elements added to non-examination courses, where many West Indian pupils, in particular, were to be found. Most of this kind of work was found only in multiracial schools and gained further momentum in such schools after the 'moral panic' over muggings and black youth in the mid 1970s (see Hall, 1978).

This kind of approach to multicultural education rested on the assumption that the poor performance and alienation in school of black and Asian children could be remedied by improving their self-images. This could be accomplished through showing respect for the cultures of ethnic minorities in the curriculum of the school.

However, Stone (1981) questions the existence of low black and Asian self-images, often finding the opposite when researching among such pupils, and suggested that the stress should really be placed on teaching basic skills more effectively. Mullard (1981) regards this type of multiculturalism as an exercise in social control, serving to contain black rebellion against a racist society by defusing pupil resistance. The changes in curriculum of some multiracial schools were, according to Troyna and Williams (1986), to make the experience of black students in education more palatable.

What critics of this kind of multiculturalism focused on was the avoidance of confronting racism at school and in society in general, a racism which black and Asian children experienced daily, and which had a detrimental effect on their life chances. It was this issue which was to stimulate further development, but, before detailing those changes in emphasis and ideology, it is important to note the changes also taking place in official thinking during this stage.

The late 1970s saw a change in emphasis in official DES documents, which now seemed to acknowledge the diversity of cultures as a permanent feature of British society. The education system and teachers should take notes that:

> Our society is a multicultural, multiracial one and the curriculum should reflect a sympathetic understanding of the different cultures and races that now make up our society. (DES, 1977, para. 10.11)

However, the kind of curriculum developments that awareness of this had led to resulted in the Home Affairs Committee (1981) commenting that a 'black studies' curriculum could become an educational ghetto for black pupils, and it urged further consideration of a suitable and relevant curriculum for a multicultural society.

The under-achievement of ethnic minority pupils, especially pupils of West Indian origin, became well documented during the 1970s, and this led the Government to set up a Committee of Inquiry in 1979 that became known as the Rampton Committee. An interim report was made in 1981, which pointed out that schools needed to take a positive attitude to the richness a culturally diverse society could offer. As Craft (1981b) notes, 1981 can now be seen as a crucial year in that not only were there four major reports on the subject as well as numerous conferences, but also there were major urban disturbances in areas of many cities of Britain with high concentration of ethnic minorities.

Lynch (1986a) notes that it is from this time that 'pluralism becomes acceptable' as part of an ideology that would seek greater social cohesion and in which the education system had a vital role to play.

The Rampton Committee report (1981) came as a disappointment to the growing number of critics of multicultural education because all that emerged on the issue of racism was that schools had a duty to combat the ignorance 'on which much racial prejudice and discrimination is based' (p. 34). The Rampton inquiry had internal disputes over the issue, which led to resignations and the appointment of a new chairman in Lord Swann, who was to complete the inquiry.

It was during the late 1970s that some LEAs, such as ILEA and Manchester, began to respond to the presence of ethnic minorities by the adoption of specific policies. These were often the result of activity in the black and Asian communities, many of which were beginning to set up alternative schooling as a means of dealing with the under-achievement of young people and the racism they experienced. In Berkshire, the county was reported to the Commission for Racial Equality on the allocation of school places within the LEA and there was a lengthy inquiry.

Gibson (1976) refers to the earlier policies as 'benevolent multi-culturalism', as their main feature was educational programmes that would ensure greater compatibility between home and school and improve performance in schools by the use of culturally relevant materials. Other LEAs adopted policies based on a notion of cultural understanding which sought to involve pupils in a process of appraisal and change regarding attitudes to and valuing of ethnic groups. (These policies and others will be examined in more detail later in this chapter.)

Both models, however, ignore the existence of racism in Britain and its institutions. In the words of the Institute of Race Relations (1980), these models 'tinker with educational techniques and methods and leave unaltered the racist fabric of the education system' (p. 82).

5 ANTI-RACISM – FROM SARIS AND SAMOSAS TO STRUGGLE

Despite the campaigns in many black and Asian communities against racism, many LEAs would still not place the matter on their agenda. This led to the creation of several pressure groups such as NAME (National Anti-racist Movement in Education) and ALTARF (All London Teachers Against Racism and Fascism), which along with black and Asian academics, began to tease out examples of racism in school practices, such as streaming or referral procedures (see Coard, 1971 and Tomlinson, 1982). Materials such as text books also began to be examined for any racist bias and a Eurocentric perspective (see Hicks, 1981 and Klein, 1982). Not all of these enquiries were published. Dawn Gill's *Assessment in a Multicultural Society: Geography* was rejected by the Schools Council for the way in which she focused on racism being perpetuated in Geography texts and other materials (see Troyna and Williams, 1986, p. 25).

The late 1970s and early 1980s also saw reports and research confirm the existence of racism in the wider society. The PEP (Political and Economic Planning) research (Smith, 1977) and (Brown, 1984) revealed the continuing extent of discrimination in employment and housing. The 1981 Home Office Report on Racial Attacks showed that racial victimisation of Asians was 50 times higher than that of white people and 36 times higher for West Indians. The report noted that many Asians now regarded racial abuse and violence as a common but unwelcome feature of British life. Discriminatory practices and overt and covert racism were revealed in other institutions, such as the police (see Smith, 1983). Leaks from the delayed Commission for Racial Equality study into immigration rules showed that whereas 1 in 140 visitors from the New Commonwealth was refused entry, 1 in 1,400 from the Old Commonwealth (mainly white) was refused entry. Their conclusion was that the immigration rules were racist in operation.

This period had also seen further controls placed on Commonwealth Immigration through Acts of Parliament in 1968 and 1971. At the same time, race relations legislation was also passed (1965, 1968 and 1976). It was not until the 1976 Act that both direct and indirect discrimination on the basis of colour, race and ethnicity were included as well as coverage of the education system. Lynch (1986b) refers to these responses as examples of Britain's 'Janus-faced' attitude to ethnic minorities. Further tensions and accusations of racism were caused by the passing of the 1981 Nationality Act, which created three distinct categories of British citizen: those born in the UK or to UK parents, citizens of dependencies (like the Falklands), and those born in former colonies. Only the first category had automatic right of entry to the UK and these were, of course, mainly white.

The weight of evidence and argument produced a climate in which it was possible for some LEAs to take a positive stance against racism. Policies began to be formulated not on the basis of cultural understanding but rather on the need for equality and social justice, involving the combating and dismantling of racism in all its forms, personal and institutional. LEA policy statements called on the schools themselves to submit and publicly declare policy statements opposing racism. They called on schools to review their practices and procedures especially in dealing with racist bullying, abuse and attacks and also to review their curriculum along anti-racist guidelines outlined by the authority and their advisers. Berkshire and ILEA were early examples of this development in 1983, followed by other LEAs, such as Bradford and Birmingham.

These policies marked the first real attempts at a more racialised concept of the nature of schooling and society and the black and Asian experience within that. As a result, anti-racism came to be seen as a radical political movement because of its emphasis on inequality and the need to understand the roots of British racism, which lay in the economic system of both the past and the present. The implication that white teachers were colluding in the perpetuation of an unequal racist society did not always go down well with educators and politicians, who professed a political and ideological neutrality.

6 ANTI-RACIST MULTICULTURALISM – A PRACTICAL SYNTHESIS?

During the early to mid-1980s there developed a polarisation of perspectives, with the continued promotion of 'black perspectives' in the curriculum arising out of the concerns and demands of black and Asian parents and educationalists. Such perspectives focused on an understanding of racism as a central feature of British society and the need for schools to develop strategies to challenge and dismantle racist practices. It also sought to make connections with structural inequalities relating to gender and class. Anti-racism was seen as a radical departure from multicultural education, which was attempting to promote racial harmony on the basis of an understanding and appreciation of other cultures. However, by 1984 Francis was making the point that 'anti-racist teaching can co-exist with a more politicised form of multicultural education' (p. 87).

Grinter (1985) voiced a growing feeling that the conflict between multicultural education and anti-racist education was 'doing great damage to the shared purpose of education for a more just society' and that 'potential allies are denouncing each other's purposes, frustrating each other's efforts and alienating potential sympathisers' (p. 7).

Grinter goes on to argue for an anti-racist multiculturalism because:

> Multicultural and anti-racist education are essential to each other. They are logically connected and each alone is inadequate. Each is appropiate to different stages and contents in education and must be part of a combined strategy if either is to have any real effect. (p. 7)

Grinter acknowledges that the kind of synthesis he is talking of is difficult, as the two positions are different in nature, one being descriptive, the other analytical; one emphasises the social and cultural aspects, the other the economic and political; one persuades, the other challenges. Despite the difficulties, it must be attempted, otherwise as Grinter fears, anti-racism's full-frontal attack on education will be seen as too political and over-sensitive. Schools will have little difficulty in seeing it off and 'the baby of multicultural practice, whatever its defects, will be swept away with the bathwater of anti-racism' (p. 8).

In supporting Grinter's approach, Mal Leicester (1986) identifies three distinct approaches taken by multicultural educators: firstly, the 'consensitive' (integrationalist) method, which draws on material from minority cultures but leaves everything as it is; secondly, the liberal approach, which sees multicultural education as a way to a genuine 'internal' understanding of a variety of traditions; thirdly, a radical approach, which is about changing the structures of education to promote equality (of outcome) for all children, regardless of race, class or gender. She argues that:

> The point is that it is not anti-racist education and multicultural education that are alternative forms of education, but that there are alternative forms of multicultural education – racist and anti-racist.

It is, of course, the latter that must be pursued.

Craft and Klein (1986) stress that 'multicultural and anti-racist education are interlocking parts of one whole, each is essential, neither is sufficient on its own' (p. 6). Support among future teachers for such an approach was shown in a study by Antonouris and Richards (1985). They studied the views of student teachers on racial education. What emerged as the most popular approach was a joint multicultural and anti-racist perspective and support for this increased during the BEd. course.

The implications of this phase are that it may well be the most appropriate approach for schools in predominantly white areas which have not yet considered the ethnocentric nature of their curriculum, let alone the issue of racism. It will not, however, be an approach without its critics.

The response of the education system to the presence of ethnic minorities in Britain has so far passed through six overlapping phases. Each of these led to certain policies being adopted. Troyna and Williams (1986) argue that this has been accompanied by a move away from 'discoursive deracialisation' (see Miles, 1982 and 1984 and Reeves, 1983). The term refers to those situations in which people talk of racist matters, whilst avoiding the overt use of racial descriptions, evaluation and prescriptions. This can justify racial discrimination by appearing to give non-racist criteria for the different treatment meted out to different racial groups.

This was the case with policies in education during phases one to four, whereas the two more recent phases show a move to benign racialisation or discoursive racialisation. This shows a growing awareness of and indignation at racial injustice and seeks to identify where and to what extent this occurs, and how to develop strategies to overcome or improve the situation.

Most of the phases outlined above included policies directed at the perceived needs of ethnic minorities in multiracial schools, rather than an improvement in education for all pupils. There was rarely any broader education justification offered for changing the curriculum or practices of all-white schools. Research by Little and Willey (1981) and Troyna and Bell (1985) showed that Heads and teachers in ethnically homogenous schools saw multicultural education as irrelevant to them and their pupils. The Swann Report (1985) concluded that this attitude 'contributed to the generally disappointing degree of progress in this field, especially in "all-white" areas' (p. 316).

The Swann Report was finally published in 1985. Its title, *Education for All*, announced how far it had moved since the inception of the inquiry in 1979, when the main concern was the under-achievement of ethnic minority pupils. Although this was dealt with and the differential IQ debate was laid to rest, the report had broadened its scope and understanding of the whole issue. It is perhaps worth remembering what the main recommendations of the report were:

> The essential steps on the argument for our concept of 'Education for All' are as follows:
>
> a) The fundamental change that is necessary is the recognition that the problem facing the education system is not how to educate children of ethnic minorities, but how to educate *all* children.
>
> b) Britain is a multi-racial and multi-cultural society and all pupils must be enabled to understand what this means.
>
> c) This challenge cannot be left to the separate and independent initiatives of LEAs and schools; only those with experience of substantial numbers of ethnic minority pupils have attempted to tackle it, though the issue affects all schools and pupils.
>
> d) Education has to be something more than the reinforcement of the

beliefs, values and identity which each child brings to school.

e) It is necessary to combat racism, to attack inherited myths and stereotypes, and the ways in which they are embodied in institutional practices.

f) Multi-cultural understanding has also to permeate all aspects of a school's work. It is not a separate topic that can be welded on to existing practices.

g) Only in this way can schools begin to offer anything approaching the *equality of opportunity* for all pupils which must be the aspiration of the education system to provide.

Verma (1989) comments that for the first time the report made it clear that the issues and needs of ethnic minorities are tied up with the education of white children, and that the notion of diversity in unity, which the report was promoting, was a bold challenge to the education system.

Although interpreted in this way by some, there were others who saw the whole exercise rather differently. For instance, Gurmah (1987) saw Swann as irrelevant to black and Asian people and the fight against racism. It was seen as a way of placating the feelings of injustice among black people by convincing them that something was being done about the situation. It was no more than a symbolic gesture and teachers should have nothing to do with this latest sop from the State.

Other professionals gave the report a mixed reception. The recognition of the missing 'all-white' dimension' and the research which accompanied it was welcomed, along with the research on the way pupils from different ethnic backgrounds experiencd the same lesson and teacher. One of the major disappointments was for those who hoped to see the encouragement of mother-tongue teaching in schools. The report recognised the importance of this but placed the major responsibility for maintenance on the community.

The disappointment many felt with the report often related to its lack of a unifying perspective, as at times it appeared to nod in the direction of anti-racism and at other times in the direction of multiculturalism. This was perhaps compounded by Lord Swann's summary, which not so much disappointed as angered many, including those on the committee. This was due to Lord Swann's view that 'race' was an invalid biological concept. His summary refused to acknowledge 'racism' as a valid socially constructed concept which impinged directly on the lives of black people. Consequently, to many black and Asian people this appeared to devaluate their experiences, while letting the perpetrators off the hook. This still remains one of the most contentious aspects of the Swann Report and certainly helped to cloud some of its more positive recommendations.

In a useful contribution to the debate, Parekh (1989) argues that reports like the Swann Report are often approached with wrong expectations, and people are invariably disappointed. These reports are, after all, written by a committee, which is often limited by its terms of reference. They are not meant to be the last word on the issue but are discussion documents for government and, in this case, LEAs and schools. However, perhaps it is only right that people do have such high expectations of a high-status inquiry which sat for five years at taxpayers' expense. The strength of the critique that follows often adds to the quality of the debate.

Despite these reservations and sharp criticisms of the Swann Report, teachers, schools, training colleges and LEAs did make use of the report and the initiatives that followed. It legitimised the work of mainly white schools and LEAs, and encouraged policy formation and expenditure. More black and Asian professionals became involved in the in-service training of those colleagues in predominantly white schools, and more concern was directed at the recruitment and use of ethnic minority teachers. Under the Education Support Grant scheme many LEAs set up projects to address the missing 'all-white dimension', identified so clearly in the full report as having been badly neglected.

Before examining how such areas and schools should and could have responded to the multicultural nature of British society, it may be useful to look at some of the early responses made by multiracial LEAs, schools and teachers, as well as some of the assumptions on which they have been based.

THE RESPONSE OF SCHOOLS AND LEAS

Many of the early curriculum innovations came from teachers themselves. For example, Tulse Hill School in 1971 developed a course, initially for sixth formers, on immigration, followed by courses for other pupils on the history of cultures of the Caribbean, Africa and Asia. William Penn School developed a 'black studies' syllabus, mainly for children of West Indian origin. Underpinning many of these courses was the notion of compensation 'for inadequacies of understanding, lack of identity and poor self-image' (Pollack, 1972, p. 10). Many schools in multiracial areas were adopting a practice of what Nixon (1985) terms 'accretion', whereby extraneous matter is added to an existing curriculum structure. This can take several practical forms. It can appear as a formal or informal optional extra through GCSE courses or an after-school 'Black Studies Club'. Or it may be part of a common core and integrated with work in Moral Education. Finally, it may appear as piecemeal development, where multicultural aspects and racism are featured in some subjects, such as English or Home Economics. The disadvantage, as many teachers and others saw it, was that multiculturalism became compartmentalised, having little impact on the ethnocentric nature of the rest of the curriculum, and that it frequently sidestepped the issue of racism.

Bullivant (1981) summarises the key assumption underlying this type of multicultural education as:

1 By learning about his/her culture and ethnic roots, an ethnic minority child will improve his/her achievement.

2 Learning about his/her culture will improve equality of opportunity.

3 Learning about other cultures will reduce children's and adults' prejudice and discrimination.

Despite the lack of evidence that multicultural education could do any of this, LEAs began to base policies on such questionable assumptions. ILEA's document (1984) stressed the need for cultures to be 'respected, differences recognised and individual identities secure' (p. 4). Manchester's document (1980) emphasised the need to combat the ignorance about cultural minorities as a way of improving relations between races. Not only were such policies criticised theoretically, they were also condemned by members of ethnic minority groups, usually for the failure to include the issue of racism.

This criticism led some LEAs to a 'paradigm shift' (Kimberley, 1986) from phase four to five. The policies of Berkshire and ILEA (1984) saw the issue no longer in terms of under-achievement or low self-image, but rather in terms of white racism. This manifested itself in racist ideologies, practices and structural inequalities. The idea that under-achievement was due to cultural differences or deprivation was attacked, as such explanations served to legitimise existing power differences. Policies reflected the aim that insitutions need to change through a close examination of the formal and hidden curriculum, assessments, streaming, staffing and how racist incidents were dealt with. To have any effect on the pattern of racial inequality, it was argued, the emphasis should be on equality of outcome rather than the equality of access (Hatcher and Shallice, 1983).

Multicultural education had no effect on under-achievement and some critics saw it as part of State policy (see Carby, 1982) to control and contain the resistance of black youth. Anti-racism, as it became known, was seen as the radical alternative to multiculturalism, challenging all types of racism and championing racial equality and justice.

ILEA's (1983) anti-racist statement committed the authority to the elimination of racism, suggesting that all its educational institutions follow a process which included:

1 Placing the issue on the school/college agenda and making time for discussion and development.

2 Coming to grips with what racism is and its historical context.

3 Considering how racism can and does operate in the school/ college.

4 Analysing both directly conscious racist behaviour and what the Rampton Interim Report termed 'unconscious racism'.

5 Analysing both individual behaviour and the policies and practices of the school/college.

6 Analysing the behaviour and practices of individuals and services that impinge on the life of the school/college.

7 Drawing upon the advice and experience of others.

Guidelines were also issued to schools to determine their own policies, which would include:

1 A clear, unambiguous statement of opposition to any form of racism or racist behaviour.

2 A firm expression of all pupils' or students' rights to the best possible education.

3 A clear indication of what is not acceptable and the procedures, including sanctions to deal with any transgressions.

4 An explanation of the way in which the school or college intends to develop practices which both tackle racism and create educational opportunities, which make for a cohesive society where diversity can flourish.

5 An outline of the measures by which developments will be monitored and evaluated.

The ILEA statement identified several areas in the life and work of the school that could contribute to tackling the racism and improve education for all.

The first of these was the ethos and climate of the school, by which the school, through assemblies and tutor-group activities, could emphasise the pluralist nature of society.

The curriculum should seek to create an understanding of an interest in different environments, societies, systems and cultures, noting the achievements made outside the western world. An historic appreciation is argued for in understanding the entrenched nature of racism due to colonial exploitation, slavery and repression, together with the ways in which this may openly and unintentionally influence curriculum content. Materials should be assessed for racism and negative stereotyping (a process which had, of course, been going on for many years).

There was encouragement to recruit more black and Asian teachers, and to examine institutional racism and how this might operate through the organisation of the school in relation to the grouping, selection and promotion of teachers.

The attitudes of staff also needed to be examined, especially the ways in which they related to expectations and stereotyping of ethnic minority pupils, with the possible result of a self-fulfilling prophesy.

Other important ways of tackling the issue were the improvement of relationships with parents and the community and the development of in-service training.

Berkshire's statement, 'Education for Racial Equality', also published in 1983, was in similar vein to that of ILEA, but attempted to clarify the ideas of equality and justice in the following way:

There will be perfect racial equality in Britain if and when Asian and Afro-Caribbean people participate fully in society and the economy

... and are not disproportionately involved in menial work or unemployment. (p. 5)

It went on to stress the importance in this process of the recruitment of more ethnic minority teachers and administrators, as well as better representation in 'stream, sets, classes and schools leading to higher and further education'. On racial justice it said:

There will be racial justice in education if and when the factors determining successful learning in schools do not discriminate directly or indirectly against ethnic minority children. (p. 5)

The general policy statement urged the 'dismantling' of racism, to be replaced by justice and equality.

Some schools attempted to follow these guidelines, mainly in multiracial urban areas. A survey by Little and Willey (1983) of 225 multiracial schools revealed that in 68 per cent of these schools the issues were raised with senior staff. In schools where 30 per cent of the pupils were from ethnic minority groups, such discussions took place in 90 per cent of schools. At department level, ways of responding to ethnic and cultural diversity were being considered by 90 per cent of English Departments, 80 per cent of History Departments, 60 per cent of Geography Departments and 40 per cent of Biology Departments. The authors noted that this level of debate was a considerable increase on that found in the early 1970s and the type of curriculum development was also different. It was less concerned with adding or replacing content and more to do with approaches to the curriculum as a whole.

This process is reflected in the activities of those schools which have made attempts at curriculum developments for a multicultural society. At Birley High School, a working party was set up to examine the 'whole work and ethos of the school in the light of its multicultural nature'. After two years of detailed consideration, it produced proposals which covered teachers attitudes and expectations, social education, tutor-group work, assemblies, syllabuses, examinations and community contact.

In conjunction with this kind of review, such schools have also produced letters of explanation to parents and general policy statements, such as that of the Skinners Company School, which says:

The Governors and staff welcome the multi-ethnic nature of present day British society and are wholly opposed to racism. We condemn all expressions of racist attitudes, either through remarks or conduct and we hope that parents and pupils will think it right to adopt a similar attitude.

Their statement also includes the following:

The curriculum should reflect the various cultures of Britain ... All racial incidents and attacks, whether physical or verbal, should be dealt with according to the clear school policy.

Such statements usually lay down a specific code or procedure to be followed in dealing with racist incidents, which include physical assault, derogatory name-calling, racist graffiti and provocative racist material and insignia. For example, at North Westminster School, the procedure following a racist incident is:

1 Report to Head of school site;

2 Head of school site records in serious incident book;

3 Full report to Headmaster/Mistress;

4 Full report to parent/guardian;

5 Support for teacher(s) concerned and victim(s);

6 Follow-up to prevent recurrence.

Schools such as Quintin Kynaston and Mayfield have their own racist incident book or referral form. It could be interpreted that the result of all this is to drive racism underground or suppress it but, as Quintin Kynaston's policy puts it:

Our aim in discussing racism with students and parents should be to positively influence them through discussion ... The first aim ... is to demonstrate that we regard all students as being of equal value.

Although the Swann Report did not endorse an anti-racist approach, it did quote with approval the kind of work done in schools as described above and some LEA statements and guidelines.

The Swann Committee noted the change in climate in the discussion of racism, which had initially produced reactions of anger, distress and defensiveness in the profession. Most people now seemed able to accept racism as 'a concept which justifies full and careful consideration' and to consider the possibility that 'certain attitudes and procedures may work against particular ethnic minority groups in society' (p. 10). The chapter on racism concludes that both individual racism and any institutional practice or procedures that reinforce such attitudes need to be tackled in the interest of the community as a whole. This is later embodied in the committee's conclusions and recommendations (p. 769).

The committee became aware at first hand of the overt and covert forms of racism within education. They 'ceased to be surprised when, even in multiracial areas and schools, pupils and teachers refer to all non-white ethnic minorities collectively as "Pakis" and their language as Indian or African' (p. 15). They experienced the widespread stereotyped expectations of West Indians as good at sport and not academic, Asians as hard working and well motivated, but with unrealistically high career aspirations, and the Chinese as always reserved and well behaved. The report noted that there seemed to be an 'order of merit' (p. 6) of those ethnic minorities regarded as least or most desirable for a teacher to have in his or her class, with Chinese rated highly desirable and West Indians at the opposite end of the scale.

Research commissioned for the Swann Report by Green (1985) showed how children of different ethnic groups, taught in the same multi-ethnic class by the same teacher, are likely to receive widely different educational experiences. Green suggests that this is attributable to teachers' frames of reference, which are predominantly ethnocentric and contain expectations and stereotypes based on class, gender and race. The research projects in the report indicated the complexity of the whole debate and showed that the report could not be expected to be the final word on all of the issues involved. However, in terms of a way forward, its general recommendations were to be tentatively explored.

INTO A NEW ERA

The post-Swann years did usher in a spate of reactions from LEAs and schools. The all-white dimension was to be addressed at last. One method was the establishment of 20- to 25-day multi-ethnic courses in various parts of the country, targeted at specific schools and individuals and aimed at creating agents for change in those schools.

LEAs were also invited to put in bids for Education Support Grants for specific projects which related to the need for education for cultural diversity in all-white areas. Between 1985 and 1987 about 70 projects were started, with a time span of between one and five years, costing £1,586,000. Between then and the end of 1989 a further 50 projects were begun, with almost every LEA in England and Wales having made some response to education for a multi-ethnic society. The projects vary considerably from establishing a multicultural resource centre to school twinning: from initial teacher training to intervention modes in schools or curriculum areas. For further details of many of these projects, see Tomlinson and Coulson (1988).

Many LEAs saw the Swann Report and its recommendations as a legitimising weapon in creating their own policy on anti-racist multicultural education. By the end of the 1980s, about 70 LEAs either had developed or were developing their own policies, usually in the 'multicultural language' of the Swann Report. Most of these LEAs, such as Cumbria, Hampshire and Gloucestershire, laid down general policy guidelines covering the ethos and curriculum of the school and the combating of racial discrimination. Hampshire's is fairly typical:

> Against the background of the Swann Report and as a development of the Country's statement on the curriculum, the following policy was adopted on 10th June, 1986.
>
> The Hampshire Education Service should prepare pupils and students for life in a multicultural society by developing an ethos and a curriculum which:
>
> a) reflect and value cultural diversity and turn it to advantage in enriching pupils' and students' experience and understanding of the world in which they live;
>
> b) recognise and counter racial prejudice;
>
> c) foster racial harmony and understanding amongst all in society;
>
> d) offer all pupils and students equality of opportunity and an education for life in a culturally and racially plural society.
>
> This policy should permeate the whole curriculum and find expression in all aspects of school and college life.

However, despite the fine words, not all LEAs were prepared to give the process of dissemination and implementation sufficient priority in terms of support through finance and staffing, relying heavily on ESG projects and 20-day courses. In many areas schools were left to themselves to work out how they were going to respond, with little practical guidance. Many did not bother.

Despite the patchy nature of some of these developments, the results of many of the projects in terms of curriculum developments and teacher attitudes and the continued debate were of sufficient weight to ensure the continuity of such a perspective through the National Curriculum Council. This was apparent in the remit given to the various subject working parties and the incorporation of multicultural education into the notion of the 'whole curriculum' in the 1990s. (The exact nature of the opportunities under the National Curriculum will be discussed later.)

The search for acceptable and meaningful terminology continues into the 1990s. For some there is no alternative to 'anti-racism'; for others the term now carries political implications or is too closely associated with certain incidents. 'Multiculturalism' is still seen as tokenistic and avoiding the real issue; 'anti-racist multiculturalism' is an uneasy alliance but with practical relevance. For some, such as John Rex (1989), the phrase 'equality of opportunity' should act as the umbrella term to cover issues in the areas of multiculturalism, disability, and gender, whereas some critics fear that such a blanket term will result in little progress in any of the areas, because of the sheer magnitude of the task.

Since the mid 1980s most LEAs have avoided an anti-racist label and produced multicultural documents (often for political purposes), while wanting to stress a commitment to opposing racism at an institutional and personal level. One possible way out of this dilemma in the future is indicated by Hampshire's change of labels from 'multicultural' to 'intercultural' education.

The appeal of this label to many in the 1990s is its association with Europe, being the term used within the EEC and comparatively under-used in the UK. The title is also meant to indicate a move away from solely parochial or national concerns to promoting a wider world-view of cultural diversity, which in the all-white context could provide a useful way into the curriculum. But how far does this also indicate an abandonment of concern for resolving the considerable inequalities suffered by Britain's ethnic minorities and the replacement of an Anglocentric curriculum with a Eurocentric one? The experience of the last twenty years immediately alerts us to this possibility and it is doubtful whether this really would be the case. There have been too many gains over that time and too many people are aware of the dangers of retrenchment to allow it to happen. Its appeal is likely to increase in the white highlands in the coming years.

SUMMARY

The six phases of educational response to Britain's diversity have mostly taken place in schools in multi-ethnic areas. Sometimes the response has been prompted by racist incidents in the school and the community, sometimes as a reaction to the demands of an LEA policy. Although some teachers in predominantly white areas shared an understanding of effective education in and for a multicultural society, it was not until the Swann Report that such developments really began to happen and those teachers felt a growing support from LEAs. Since the publication of the Swann Report, developments have been patchy and relatively slow, for reasons that will be discussed in later chapters. However, it is likely that in the new ERA of education with the National Curriculum, more and more schools will have to address this issue.

The purpose of this book is not simply to reassert the rationale for such developments, but to offer some practical ideas on how they may be achieved.

Developments in anti-racist multicultural education over the last two decades have not always been smooth. There have been some practitioners and academics who have had reservations about the use of many of the terms, their meaning and the implications they have for the curriculum of a school. Some have not simply resisted these ideas but have campaigned actively against them and it is these anxieties and criticisms to which I shall turn in Chapter 2.

2

Clarifying the concepts

RACISM

One criticism frequently levelled at anti-racist multicultural education is that the terminology used lacks clarity of definition and therefore can be confusing. However, terms such as racism, prejudice, pluralism, multiculturalism, institutional racism, racial equality and social justice have been the subject of intense debate in the literature of the past 15 years. There may not always have been agreement, but this is not an unusual occurrence in educational debates, especially when it involves sensitive and emotionally charged issues. The debate has never been avoided, just misrepresented, and continues to be so to this day.

'Racism' has at one time or another been seen as a doctrine which maintains that one race of people is genetically superior to another. Such 'scientific racism' has a long history within European culture, dating back to the eighteenth century. (For a succinct account of the contribution of science to the development and perpetuation of racist thought, see Milner, 1983, pp.9–15). The concept of biologically distinct 'races' is no longer accepted as valid by the majority of the scientific community (see Rose, 1984) but still lingers in the consciousness of many lay people and may inform their interaction with certain ethnic groups within Britain.

The term 'racism' has sometimes been equated with 'prejudice', racial discrimination being seen as the result of an individual's racial prejudice, which is the culmination of acquiring historical and other negative stereotypes. (Psychologists since Allport (1958) have argued that, for some individuals, racial prejudice may also fulfil a personality need which functions to explain and direct social action.) This kind of interpretation informed a lot of the Swann Report and underpinned some of the early multicultural work.

This interpretation has been frequently criticised in the subject literature over the years for the lack of any structural understanding of how racism developed from certain economic circumstances and became institutionalised for political purposes. From this perspective, racism is seen as the direct and deliberate consequence of capitalist colonial exploitation on the part of European nations and has become an overt and covert part of all their social institutions.

Thus 'racism' is seen as structurally bound up with capitalism and imperialism and the unequal relationship between black and white people. This has led some to the conclusion that because of the pervasive nature of racism, all white people are inevitable racists and that, although this could be ameliorated by means of certain kinds of training programmes, it could never be eradicated. (These programmes, their assumptions and their effectiveness will be discussed in Chapter 5). A shorthand slogan for this latter perspective was 'racism = prejudice + power'. This catchy but rather limited formula reverted to what Carter and Williams (1987) refer to as a 'personalised view of power and an understanding of racism which sets it aside from economic relations' (p. 174). In addition, it restricted an understanding of 'racism' to deliberate acts of discrimination and failed to contribute to an understanding of working-class racism.

As an explanatory framework to understand racism, this singular connection between western capitalism and racism, still put forward by some writers (such as Miles, 1988), has become increasingly difficult to maintain in the face of evidence of racist beliefs, practices and violence in countries such as Bulgaria, the Soviet Union, China and elsewhere in the world. In a review of Miles' book, Paul Rich makes the point that 'Capitalism has clearly shown in various societies a capacity opportunistically to adapt and take advantage of racist structures ...' and that '... businessmen tend to create the conditions for the emergence of racism rather than racism itself' (p. 167). 'Racism', according to Rich, is the manifestation of the relationship between economic and military power, and we need to examine this and so move beyond the phase of western liberal guilt which has characterised so much of the debate over the past decades.

The way in which the concept has been incorporated into policy documents such as ILEA's and Berkshire's is criticised by Troyna and Williams (1986) because of a crude distinction made between black and white and because 'by drawing attention to one measure of inequality (i.e. 'race') other forms of inequality (i.e. class, gender) are implicitly taken as acceptable' (p. 105).

In order to gain a clearer understanding of 'racism' we have to acknowledge:

1 That although 'race' is not a valid scientific concept, it is an important social construction, in that people have certain views and make certain assumptions about themselves and others which effect their interaction. In this process individuals will draw on previous knowledge and experience to orientate themselves in interactions. Figueroa (1984) refers to this as a person's 'racial frame of reference':

A racial frame of reference, broadly speaking, is a socially constructed, socially reproduced and learned way of orientating with and towards others and the world involving ultimately tacit assumptions such as: there do actually exist objectively different 'races'; these share ' by nature' or genetically or inherently certain common characteristics, including or closely linked with certain social characteristics; the different 'races' are mutually exclusive if not hierarchically ordered; each person belongs to one and only one such 'race', thereby possesssing certain physical and cultural characteristics and occupying a certain social location. (p. 19)

The 'racial frame of reference' will also include other ideas, myths and assumptions about other cultures and religions which derive from the culture and history of society. 'Racism is therefore more than the sum of individual prejudice: it becomes an organising principle of popular consciousness' (Carter and Williams, 1987, p. 177).

2 Racism may manifest itself in various ways in different societies under different economic and political conditions. Within Britain, Halstead (1988) identifies six types of racism which may appear alone or in combination with each other and the following is a brief summary:

a) Pre-reflective gut racism

This is based on powerful emotions which have deep psychological roots in insecurity and fear of strangers or difference, reinforced by negative racial myths. It results in acts of rejection, hostility and violence towards minority groups. It need not be confined to white Europeans but within the context of Britain it usually is.

b) Post-reflective gut racism

This is the rationalisation of practices in the above within a religious or scientific framework.

c) Cultural racism

This seeks to justify racist attitudes and practices in cultural terms. The culture of minority groups is seen as deficient in social customs, manners, appropriate attitudes, etc. and holding them back. If they refuse to turn their backs on their own culture, then any discrimination is their own fault. 'Cultural racism demands cultural conformity' (p. 146).

d) Institutional racism

This is the way in which societies' institutions operate to the continued advantage of the majority, in this case white, population, either intentionally or unintentionally. It would also include the 'racism by omission' in a school's curriculum.

e) Paternalistic racism

This refers to the actions and policies of white power-holders who believe that they know what is best for ethnic minorities. Examples would be the bussing of black children (but not white), tokenistic curricular changes, and some multicultural policies which are directed at maintaining social stability and defusing racial conflict without addressing the issue of inequalities.

f) Colour-blind racism

The commonly expressed sentiment that 'I treat them all the same' can have serious racist implications. Such an approach denies the relevance of minority groups' experiences, which will usually include racism. It thus ignores or marginalises their needs and what they bring to situations.

Once these aspects of racism have been acknowledged, it is possible to begin devising suitable strategies to address them.

Halstead argues that we must come to see racism as racial injustice and that there are definite advantages in doing so.

Firstly, racism is then related to a fundamental value of a democratic pluralistic society and is therefore of concern to all people, black/Asian and white.

Secondly, it addresses one of the points made earlier by Troyna and Williams, in that opposition to racial injustice is one manifestation of the broader issue of justice and 'is fully compatible with working for justice in other areas' (p. 159).

Thirdly, it addresses Troyna's and Williams' other point in that it avoids a simple division into black and white. Opposing racism need not mean an automatic support for black/Asian people no matter what the circumstances because the concept of justice remains a central overarching principle.

Fourthly, the understanding is not tied to a specific political ideology and so seen as the prerogative of a particular sectional interest. This does not mean that there is no place for a political solution to the question of racism.

Finally, Halstead argues that such a definition increases our awareness of the complexity of the problem and provides a suitable framework for its continual discussion.

Halstead's contribution to the debate has helped to clarify many of the issues involved in an understanding of racism. It demonstrates the concern of those involved in anti-racist multicultural education openly to confront the question of definitions, in order that appropriate action can be taken by schools to counter the development of racist attitudes and practices.

There have also been several criticisms of the kinds of policies and actions in schools and LEAs described in the last chapter. Jeffcoate (1984a) sees them as a 'retrograde step' (p.25) and declares that:

> Recent initiatives by a few local authorities and schools . . . appear to threaten the autonomy of teachers and pupils and . . . evoke the spectres of indoctrination and totalitarianism. (p. 150)

Jeffcoate sees anti-racism as anti-democratic, as it lays down quite specifically what is and is not permissible for teachers and pupils in terms of behaviour and attitude. He criticises the definition of racism which is usually employed for revealing a Marxist interpretation. However, in practice, the definition of racism employed in many LEA policies is more akin to that of Berkshire:

> Racism encompasses racialism, but refers also to institutions and routine procedures as well as to the actions of individuals and to unconscious and unintentional effects, as well as to deliberate purposes . . . which create and maintain power, influence and well being of white paper at the expense of Asian and Afro-Caribbean people. (p. 4)

Such a definition may be held without a deep commitment to Marxism. The reference to 'institutional racism' in Berkshire's definition, and in most others, is also criticised.

INSTITUTIONAL RACISM

The definition of 'institutional racism' in LEA and school anti-racist policies follows closely that of A. K. Spears (1978):

> Since it is institutionalised, all cases of racism do not result from the wilful acts of ill-intentioned individuals. It is in its most profound instances, covert, resulting from acts of indifference, omission and refusal to challenge the status quo. (p. 129)

Jeffcoate (1984a) can understand the relevance of institutional racism in the USA, where racial inequality reproduces itself over generations and has been resistant to remedial action. However, he criticises its application to Britain 'where nine out of ten of all black adults in the early 1970s were immigrants who had arrived during the previous twenty years' (p. 26). Jeffcoate implies that it is only within the past twenty years that Britain has had anything to do with immigrants from her ex-colonies, which is very misleading.

It seems inconceivable that a country which once had the largest collection of overseas colonies, over which it established certain social, economic, political and administrative structures, together with an ideological justification for the situation, should not have retained certain attitudes and practices which reveal themselves in a wide variety of forms, from political policies to use of language, even when that Empire no longer formally exists.

Jeffcoate's confusion over this is obvious (1984b) when he attempts to acknowledge and deny its existence at the same time:

> Lord Scarman . . . was evidently puzzled by the way the allegation of institutional racism kept cropping up in the evidence he received on the causes of the Brixton riots in 1981. To him, and many liberals, an institutionally racist society means one which 'knowingly, as a matter of policy, discriminates' against certain ethnic groups. On the basis of this definition, South Africa is such a society. Lord Scarman was quite adamant that institutional racism in this sense does not exist in Britain today. Most liberals would, I think, be inclined to agree with him, while making an exception of immigration control and the 1981 British Nationality Act, since their combined, if *unstated*, [author's

emphasis] object is to limit the number of British citizens who are not white. (p. 169)

Thus Jeffcoate will only accept the existence of institutional racism when it is done knowingly or when there is 'hard evidence' for it, as in racial discrimination in employment or racial attacks. As Mike Cole (1986) points out, 'black people have long known that racism does not only exist when white liberals claim that it does' (p. 21). In other words, providing white people don't think they are being racist, then they are not. What Cole (1986) and others say is that:

Statements like this are an insult to the black community who suffer the effects of racism in every facet of their lives. Such statements are also in themselves a form of racism. (p. 21)

Jeffcoate's attempt to deny the existence of institutional racism becomes further confused by his apparent acceptance of the 'unstated' racist effect of the British Nationality Act of 1981 and immigration controls. The operation of the latter was referred to in Chapter 1, based on the CRE's (1985) survey. Most supporters of both matters have usually presented their arguments in deracialised discourse, only those of the extreme right have justified such actions on racist grounds. Consequently, if we accept Jeffcoate's definition that institutional racism exists only when it is done knowingly, then, by these same criteria, the British Nationality Act and immigration controls are not examples of institutional racism for their racist effects are not done 'knowingly'.

However, Jeffcoate does make an exception of nationality and immigration controls. Therefore, if a society exhibits institutional racism in the process of entry and limits immigrants' future status within the 'host' nation, this must reflect the unstated views and prejudices of policy makers and power-holders, many of whom will be elected representatives of the people. Why should such attitudes and beliefs not be reflected in other institutions and practices in society?

One way in which institutional racism may operate within education is suggested by Coard (1971), who noted the disproportionate placement of West Indians in ESN schools and their overrepresentation in lower streams in schools. Research by Tomlinson (1982) has showed that, at that time, 0.5 per cent of Indian and Pakistani children and 0.6 per cent of indigenous children were in ESN schools, compared with 2.9 per cent of West Indian children.

Tomlinson found that, despite DES claims that the trend was not reversing, the current figure for West Indian pupils was still 2.5 per cent. Her study also found that it took an indigenous child about two years to pass through the assessment procedures, whereas it took only eleven months for an 'immigrant' child.

Evidence such as this has often been interpreted as 'institutional racism' and discriminatory practices, whether intended or not, have contributed to West Indian under-achievement. The debate on West Indian performance in schools is by no means clear cut, however, as there is evidence that those who stay on to the sixth form do better than their white peers, and South Asians perform very similarly, to white children in public examinations.

Jeffcoate has nothing to say on the high number of West Indian pupils in such schools, although he does not say that no-one 'knows' why there is a high proportion of West Indians in bottom sets. The argument advanced is that it probably has more to do with the fact that they are likely to be working class than with being black. Jeffcoate (1984a) also argues that, if they were distributed among and across forms and sets, this would undermine the basis 'of streaming and setting which is some kind of objective assessment' (p. 147). Thus Jeffcoate attempts to locate under-achievement within the notion of cultural discontinuity rather than the effects of racism. As a result of this, under-achievement is seen as a consequence of cultural patterns within the working class which hinder success in schools, again under-achievers are responsible for their own failure.

The assumption that setting and streaming are part of an objective assessment would be regarded today as very questionable, yet Jeffcoate ignores what has been and continues to be a major educational issue. Coard's explanation that the causes lie in unsuitable tests, low teacher expectations, teacher stereotyping and cultural bias are now more commonly accepted. These factors are recognised as contributing causes in ILEA's and Berkshire's anti-racist statements and in many school policies which seek to develop strategies for overcoming them.

The influence and importance of teacher expectations and stereotyping was also referred to in the Swann Report (1985), which suggested that this could have a detrimental effect on educational achievements, especially if it was combined with negative views of a group's academic ability and potential. It could result in a self-fulfilling prophecy.

Before Swann, Brittain (1976) noted the 'high degree of consensus' among teachers regarding the low ability and poor discipline of West Indian pupils, together with staffroom remarks of a racist character. Carrington and Woods' (1983) study of Hillsview Comprehensive illicited clear racial stereotyping from teachers who described West Indians as 'indolent', 'insolent', 'disruptive and aggressive' and 'lacking in ability'. Teachers also commented on West Indians having 'greater athletic prowess' or a 'well developed sense of artistic ability', the latter being a more sophisticated version of 'they've got natural rhythm'.

Although most of these teachers were not overtly hostile or intentionally racist, the manner in which they behaved was affected by their stereotypes and was racist in consequence.

Jeffcoate (1984a) answers the above in the following way:

> I have heard teachers say ghastly things about ethnic minorities in staffrooms and meetings . . . but what teachers say in such settings is not necessarily a reliable guide to their classroom behaviour or even perhaps to their real beliefs. (pp. 64–5)

Yet again, Jeffcoate treats an important educational issue as unproblematical. There are many on both sides of the political spectrum who would not share his high opinion of teachers' ability to leave their prejudices, stereotypes and value judgements in the staffroom pidgeon hole, especially when they may not be fully aware of the extent of their own prejudices.

The refusal of those educationalists committed to the notion of cultural pluralism to acknowledge the existence of racism, especially institutional racism, and their recent attacks on such concepts, have hindered the further development of LEA and school policies, which are attempting not only to ensure that the curriculum reflects Britain's cultural plurality, but also to try to tackle teacher attitudes and entrenched school or institutional practices. As Stuart Hall (1980) says:

> The issue of race provides one of the most important ways of understanding how this society actually works and how it has arrived where it is. It is one of the most important keys, not into the margins of the society, but to its dynamic centre. (p. 69)

Although there has been a reluctance to consider the value of concepts such as 'institutional racism', unlikely support for its existence and the necessity of dealing with it comes from the experience of the US military. In 1969, following the urban disturbances in several American cities, there followed a series of racial incidents at eleven army bases and major incidents at marine bases in Japan. Such incidents and the attitudes they revealed were obviously potentially damaging to the cohesion and effectiveness demanded of the military services. As a result, the Equal Opportunities Management Institute was set up to organise courses on race relations. By the mid 1970s, as the extent of prejudice and discriminatory behaviour and practices was revealed, the course developed into a sixteen-week 'awareness training' course and the original emphasis on personal racism was 'considerably broadened to cover also institutional racism and other aspects of discrimination' (Peppard, 1983).

The emphasis moved to one of securing equality of opportunity and justice, just as developments in many LEAs have attempted to do.

Anti-racist policies have further been criticised for threatening the autonomy of teachers and pupils, criticisms which can perhaps best be summarised as follows:

1 Why should racist behaviour in the form of graffiti, verbal abuse or physical violence be especially proscribed, i.e. is it any more reprehensible than the bullying or insults directed at those who are fat?

2 Statements such as 'I think blacks should be sent home because we are overcrowded' are not racist but the expression of a political opinion, however erroneous. Teachers can open up the statement to the discipline of evidence with correct information in the form of facts and statistics, etc.

3 Racist literature should also be regarded as the free expression of opinion.

4 The only criteria for the examination of teaching materials should be truth and accuracy.

5 Teachers should have the right to join racist organisations without the threat of dismissal, as it is their democratic right, as is their role to uphold democratic principles, even racist ideas.

6 The small minority of mainly white working-class adolescents who openly express racial hostility are not so much drawn to racist

organisations through ideology as through 'the paraphernalia of membership, the prospect of violence and the general aura of anti-establishment disreputability and defiance' (Jeffcoate, 1984a, p. 150).

Before answering these points, it is worth bearing in mind that the kinds of policies which the above six points are directed against are, in most cases, the result of actions or initiatives from practising teachers and not just educational theorists or the DES.

Few practising teachers would argue that some types of bullying are more reprehensible than others, and this is usually made clear in a school's overall policy towards discipline. However, teachers are aware that physical attacks or abuse directed at members of ethnic minority groups are not just straightforward cases of bullying. They can be seen as symbolic attacks, for a variety of reasons, on a whole group who exhibit certain 'racial' or cultural characteristics. As such, this places such incidents in a slightly different category, which justifies special attention.

The publication, distribution and oral expression of racist views have been outlawed through Race Relations Acts as a recognition that democratic freedoms entail the right of all citizens to live free from any persecution or harassment which may be directed at them because of their racial or religious origins. Schools are therefore following the spirit of recent race relations legislation in attempting to control racist abuse and literature. Indeed, many authorities, such as ILEA, have justified their actions by reference to Section 71 of the Race Relations Act 1976 which places a duty on every local authority to:

1 eliminate racial discrimination;

2 promote equality of opportunity and good relations between persons of different racial groups.

For a member of any local authority staff, especially a teacher, to belong to a racist organisation poses special problems. Most such organisations are anti-democratic, committed to an ideology of white, protestant nationalism and authoritarian rather than democratic. It would therefore be very contradictory for such a teacher to remain within an education system which espouses the ideology of liberal democracy and has a commitment to the notion of cultural pluralism.

The appeal to 'truth and accuracy' in the assessment of teaching materials is understandable and yet also reveals a certain naivety.

Such notions have to be treated with care, taking into account their cultural and historical relativity as well as the effects of an ethnocentric tradition.

A study by Cochrane and Billig (1984) threw new light on the link between young people's racist views and political sympathies and action. As well as noting the increase in *potential* support for such ideas as repatriation during a time of decline in *electoral* support for such parties, the authors also concluded that support for fascist parties 'has little to do with the actions of the fascist party leaders. Very few of these young people had any contact at all with fascist parties' (p. 255).

Cochrane and Billig also readily identified the type of pupils and students referred to by Jeffcoate who were 'frighteningly forthright' in their racist views and who 'rejoiced in their bigotry, enjoying the shock of expressing it in the crudest and most violent tones' (p. 256). More significantly, Cochrane and Billig identified an attitude which many teachers involved in the development of anti-racist and multicultural education had also noticed, and which had often acted as a spur to the development of this kind of work:

> What has become marked since the start of our study in 1979 has been the emergence of a type of fascist party supporter who does not hold the unambiguous views of the crude bigot. This type of supporter accepts, to a certain extent, the rhetoric of tolerance and admits that prejudice is wrong. The racist views are presented with a respectability that the crude bigot eschews. The believer claims to contemplate the expulsion of non-whites with reluctance, even regret, as the only way of preventing 'things' (principally unemployment and inflation) slipping further out of control. (p. 257)

Such views were not confined to working-class respondents, but were also in evidence in higher social classes. The authors describe this as a kind of 'genteel fascism'. These individuals would not assault members of ethnic minority groups, or damage their property, or abuse them verbally, and sought to distance themselves from the behaviour of the extreme right. It is this kind of attitude which many teachers in both multiracial and 'all-white' schools are trying to combat, by developing strategies and undertaking curriculum reviews. What this involves is examining accepted institutional practices and teaching materials for possible unintentional racism.

Troyna and Williams (1986) see the development of the term

'institutional racism' as the key concept in the developing racialisation of policy discourse in Britain. They locate its origin in the Black Power Movement in the USA in the 1960s, when it was used to contrast individual racism with less overt and more subtle forms of oppression, which perpetuated racial inequalities whether or not this was the intention. Thus the emphasis was placed on the consequences of actions, practices and structures. Troyna and Williams argue that its meaning has been over-simplified, reducing it to denoting a direct and casual relationship between one form of inequality and one institution. What has to be remembered is that education is only one institution involved in creating and perpetuating racial inequalities. Solutions offered in the rhetoric of anti-racist school or LEA policies will not create better housing or equal job opportunities. What they suggest is the need for a clearer definition of institutional racism, for, as they point out, 'does the presence of any form of inequality imply its existence?' (p. 55)

POLICY TERMINOLOGY

Troyna and Williams (1986) are not only concerned with influential concepts within the growing racialisation of LEA policies, but also examine policy formation, content and practice.

Their study focused on the documents and policies of seven LEAs: Berkshire, Bradford, Brent, Haringey, ILEA Manchester and Sheffield. Although these authorities are at different stages in developing their policies, it is possible to identify certain common standards and themes:

1 The policies are presented as cross-party policies with no serious disputes about their adoption.

2 This is achieved by an appeal to the tradition of tolerance in Britain and a need for all citizens to have full civil liberties.

3 It appears to have been a useful strategy for securing black/Asian votes at local level.

4 Policies, especially those which are anti-racist, are presented as a radical break with previous ones.

5 In most cases there is no clear statement specifying the exact nature of education inequalities.

6 Racism is used as a catch-all term for everything that is wrong with education and society. This embraces:

  a) a moral emphasis, which sees racism as offensive and unjustifiable, resulting in a need to raise people's consciousness;

  b) an educational emphasis, where racism is fed by ignorance, resulting in a need for an anti-racist curriculum;

  c) a political analysis, which shows the historical and contemporary manifestations of inequality and oppression;

  d) a behavioural emphasis, which stresses a need to control or change such actions in the interests of harmony.

7 A tendency for such policies to become incorporated in an Equal Opportunities policy.

8 A tendency for LEAs and their officers to move from a permissive mode of intervention, in which responsibility for implementation is devolved to Heads and teachers, to a more interventional position. Many policies call on schools and colleagues to make a public anti-racist response, often within a specific time.

9 There is also considerable vagueness regarding how a school should introduce anti-racist measures or a multicultural curriculum.

As mentioned in point 4 and Chapter 1, anti-racist policies were usually presented as a significant break with previous or existing policies. Troyna and Williams (1986), however, note that certain key words and concepts associated with an anti-racist paradigm echo the concerns of the multicultural paradigm which it is supposed to supersede. For instance, stability is threatened in both paradigms. In the anti-racist paradigm it is by racist groups or views and, in the multicultural paradigm, by alienation of black pupils. Harmony is threatened by black resistance to racism and under-achievement in the anti-racist paradigm, so there is a need to challenge racism. Justice is seen as the acquisition and practice of full civil and political rights. Greater racial equality in this matter is necessary for a cohesive democracy. Truth is derived solely from a white ethnocentric school curriculum, giving a false view of identity and breeding ignorance on which prejudice and racism can feed.

Troyna and Williams conclude from this that anti-racist policies 'do not constitute a radical break from earlier educational concerns. On the contrary, they have been the staple diet of educational policies for at least three decades' (p. 91).

In examining the concerns and the use of language to express these, Troyna and Williams adopt the notion of 'condensation symbols' developed by Edelman (1964). This is the use of certain words or phrases, the deliberate political purpose of which is to create symbolic stereotypes and metaphors to reassure supporters that their interests have been considered, although the words or phrases may in fact also have contradictory meanings.

As already mentioned, ideas of harmony and stability feature in most anti-racist policies, usually connected to a notion of a 'plural' or 'multicultural' society. This term is usually used as both a descriptive and an ideal prescriptive term so that the difference between what society is and what it should be like is in fact lost, as well as how earnestly we should strive for it. There is an emphasis on existing structural racial inequalities and the ideal to which we may strive, without explaining how these are related to the education system. One assumption which underlies many of these policies is that education is the main determinant of life chances and consequently the main source of all inequalities in life and society. Troyna and Williams (1986) conclude that:

> What is required in these policies is more emphasis in the initial analysis on the education system, an acknowledgement of its limited role in the perpetuation of racial inequalities in the UK and a linking passage which paves the way for a focus on specific educational concerns. (p. 101)

A second 'condensation symbol' identified is the idea of justice in LEA policies, which is taken to mean a range of citizenship rights, from the right not to be abused physically or verbally because of the colour of one's skin, to the more complex right to have one's history and culture reflected in a respectful and non-tokenistic manner in the school curriculum. Apart from the practical difficulty of how to establish such a notion of justice, there are also other implications. Troyna and Williams (1986) make the point that such a focus on racial injustices suggests that it is only these which are unacceptable and that other inequalities based on class or gender remain untouched and unlinked.

Equality is another term frequently used in these LEA policies. It usually refers to equality of outcome, as in Berkshire's policy:

> There will be perfect racial equality in Britain if and when Asian and Afro-Caribbean people participate fully in society and the economy and are therefore proportionately involved in management and government at all levels and are not disproportionately involved in manual work or in unemployment or underemployment. (p. 5)

Policies such as Berkshire's imply that to achieve equality of outcome necessitates an increase in equality of opportunity. However this is not to be achieved by positive discrimination or affirmative action. As Berkshire's policy states:

> the statement is not recommending positive discrimination . . . it does not envisage that membership of an ethnic minority could ever be a reason, in itself, for treating one individual more favourably than another. (p. 3)

Consequently, how equality of outcome is to be achieved and the school's part in this is left rather vague.

Although racism is presented as a 'white problem', it is located within a framework of black and Asian needs which require special treatment, such as under-achievement, disruptive behaviour, language, and so on. The implication and effect of policies such as these has been to imply that it is only those schools which have ethnic minority pupils who need to challenge racism and review their curriculum and practices. As Troyna and Williams conclude:

> The vexed question of how and why anti-racist education might relate to the activities and procedures of teachers in 'all-white' schools highlights most vividly the serious omissions from and the contradictions in LEA anti-racist education policies. (p. 109)

It is that particular question which the latter part of this book will deal with.

PLURALISM, CULTURE AND CURRICULUM CONTENT

The essential problem that education and society have to resolve is to establish, as Craft (1984) points out, the 'minimum level of acculturation necessary for full participation in society and the maximum extent to which diversity might be encouraged' (p. 16). This 'pluralist dilemma', as Bullivant (1981) called it, raises the question of the role of education in a democratic, industrial and culturally plural society. How far can diversity be pursued when one of the main roles of education is the fostering of social cohesion? What selection of cultures are to be included in the curriculum? By what criteria are they to be selected and by whom? How is all this to be taught? These are the kinds of questions raised in the debate but not always addressed.

Bullivant (1984) notes that the concept of cultural pluralism is plagued with ambiguity, generality and confusion. Gundara (1986) states that terms such as 'multicultural' and 'multiracial' are 'commonly ill defined'. Modgil (1986) states at the very beginning of the book, aptly subtitled 'The Interminable Debate', that 'confusion and contradiction permeate multicultural education' (p. 1). This has led Grant (1984) to comment that 'declaring in favour of multicultural education is as easy and as limited as declaring in favour of virtue' (p. 19).

These conceptual difficulties have often meant that important questions about the philosophy and practice of multicultural education are avoided.

Grant and Sleeter (1985) reviewed 200 journal articles on multicultural education. They concluded that:

1 There was lacking a clear idea of what kind of society advocates were seeking.

2 There was little use of social science theory in the search for this.

3 There was a lack of agreement on the approach needed in schools for change.

4 Many of the guidelines for multicultural education were left to the imagination of the schools.

The authors also noted an absence of dialogue between teachers, professionals and administrators on multicultural education. There was also very little evidence of any evaluation of what multicultural education actually is in practice at the classroom level. In only three of the nineteen studies they came across did the research involve entering classrooms.

As a result, multicultural education has developed in a haphazard way, often being reduced to the cultural artefacts model, i.e. the three 'S's, and often justified on the grounds of improving the self-image of ethnic minority pupils.

An underlying assumption of this practice is that education's role is to foster critical reflection, imagination, pupils' ability to weigh up evidence and become free from prejudice, to encourage a respect for others, humility, objectivity and the truth. It is from this perspective that Jeffcoate launched his attack on anti-racism's concepts and implications. It is a practice which believes that learning about others' language, religion, social structures and history will engage pupil sympathies and affection as they learn to value the richness of the unity and diversity of human beings. However, as Parekh (1986) remarks, this is 'sociologically naive' (p. 20). It ignores the social context of education and its practice. Pupils do not come to school ignorant of other cultures or peoples. They have views formed from family, media and personal experience, which continues during their time at school. Not all are negative, but many pupils will reject the school's notion of multiculturalism or reinterpret its content if it conflicts with what is learnt in the home. Thus racist and sexist stereotypes can be perpetuated. This is in part due to a reluctance to recognise the existence of racism and its effects on the life chances of ethnic minority pupils.

Banks (1986) attempts to place multicultural education in an historical context when he points out that, during the early years, such an education is likely to develop a variety of forms as it defines its boundaries and principles. During this time its concepts are likely to be violated by its practitioners. Banks comments that 'rather than analysing the goals of the movement as stated by its theorists or describing the best school practices, the critics have chosen some of the worst practices masquerading as multicultural education. The critics create straw men whom they then destroy' (p. 225).

Banks also acknowledges that there is a wide gulf between theory and practice and that this, along with the unresolved questions, needs to be tackled. Later chapters of this book will deal with these questions.

Developing a multicultural curriculum which positively embraces cultural diversity and combats racism means accepting that different value systems have equal meaning within their own context. It entails a rejection of absolutes and a recognition that cultures are different, but that none is inherently superior or inferior to another. It means an acceptance of the tentative nature of knowledge, uncertainty, disagreement and diversity. What this implies is the rejection of the notion of education as the transmission of 'high culture', or an initiation into intrinsically worthwhile activities, and as access to the seven forms of knowledge (Peters, 1965; Hirst, 1965). For this means the existence and desirability of just one perspective, which in reality will be a reflection of the ideology of the dominant group in society. It also has the implication of suggesting the existence of superior and inferior cultures.

Most contemporary social scientists view culture as something more than just tradition, language, arts and religion which is transmitted via education to the next generation. There is more of an emphasis on the symbolic, ideational and intangible aspects of group life, with some going as far as to exclude artefacts from the definition. Those that do include artefacts stress that it is the way people interpret, use, value and perceive material objects which is the distinguishing factor between peoples as much as the artefacts and traditions themselves. Sachs (1986) argues that multiculturalists have often operated with 'naive and outdated static conceptions of culture' which have given rise to the exotic tokenistic approaches.

Culture should be seen as 'knowledge' on which individuals draw to make sense of their day-to-day lives and this will be mediated through gender, class, age, time and place. Any attempt to incorporate 'multicultural' perspectives in the curriculum will have to take account of this in planning, delivery and monitoring.

A multicultural curriculum implies a view of education as a process of individual growth. In this process the attributes focused on are critical awareness, respect for others and the ability to exercise some control over one's life. Consequently curriculum selection is made on the basis of what forms of development we should encourage in order to prepare pupils for life in a multicultural society. It takes full account of pupils' knowledge and language in order to demonstrate the valuing of the pupils' own culture. This does not mean trapping pupils within their own culture, therefore limiting their intellectual and social horizons. It entails exposing pupils to a variety of value systems, encouraging them to explore them, question them and develop their own responses to them.

Jeffcoate (1979) attempted to identify the kind of criteria which could be used in the difficult task of selecting learning experiences which would result in a curriculum that should:

1 Be international in its choice of content and global in its perspective.

2 Reflect the variety of social and ethnic groups in contemporary Britain in the visual and textual information conveyed to children.

3 Convey accurate information about racial and cultural differences and similarities.

4 Present individuals from different British minority groups as individuals with every variety of human quality and attribute.

5 Allow other cultures and nations to have their own validity and be described in their own terms rather than in British or European terms and norms.

These criteria have been developed further by Cohen and Manion (1985) under the two headings of 'Respect for Others' and 'Respect for Self', suggesting numerous objectives under cognitive knowledge, cognitive skills and affective attitudes, values and emotional sets. These aims are summarised by Page and Thomas (1984) when they write:

> Multicultural education for white children can be justified by the need to prepare for life in a multicultural society, by the need for the curriculum to reflect the multicultural society, by the desirability of an enriched curriculum and the need to promote more positive race relations. (p. 44)

In a culturally plural society there is the difficulty of what precisely should be selected from a group's culture. Zec (1980) warns of the dangers of relativism and the sentimental valuing of all aspects of a culture which are different from the teacher's. A multicultural curriculum must therefore not suspend critical judgement on certain practices in another culture as long as they are seen from the perspective of that culture as well. Nor does it mean passing on lumps of a variety of cultures. Willey (1984) argues that what a multicultural curriculum is attempting to develop in children is the ability to deal with the diversity of human ideas, achievements and experiences so they can be viewed without prejudicial assumptions. Nor does it mean that whatever is included in the curriculum remains there forever. Whatever is selected in a multicultural curriculum is under constant evaluation, open to amendment or rejection. This will continue to develop as more members of ethnic minorities demand a say in the process and, as the number of teachers from ethnic minority backgrounds increases, the evaluation procedures them-selves will come under scrutiny.

There are two major factors which emerge from this. Firstly, a multicultural curriculum is not an 'anything goes' curriculum. Secondly, all the values of all cultural groups in society cannot have an equal place in a multicultural curriculum. There is, therefore, a need for guidelines on the selection of content.

Banks (1976) has produced a list of 23 guidelines which attempt to identify the underlying principles as a basis for decisions about the shape and content of a systematic whole-school approach to multicultural education. He insists (1981) that such an education 'is designed for all students of all races' (p. 30). Banks goes on to offer detailed evaluation guidelines for multicultural education.

In order that these guidelines may be placed within a more coherent framework, Lynch (1986a) has attempted a comprehensive definition of multicultural education to which the guidelines should be addressed:

> Multicultural education is an education appropriate to a multicultural society. A multicultural society is one where there is a legitimately accepted diversity of cultural appurtenances, based on such dimensions as race, colour, language, creed, sex, class, region etc. and committed to the basic ethnic of 'respect for persons' [it is therefore] against racism, sexism, creedism etc. (p. 95)

The dilemma expressed here again is, as Craft (1984) notes, how far education for diversity can be taken before social cohesion in a highly industrialised and democratic society is put at risk. Craft goes on to argue that this 'dilemma' is not really new as cultural pluralism has existed in Britain for centuries and, in fact, exists in most societies. It is difficult to find a society with a homogenous culture. There are in most societies religious variations, urban/rural, town/city, highland/lowland regional variations; sub-cultures based on age, social classes with distinctive life styles and life chances, and vertical divisions of ethnicity. According to Krejil and Velimsky (1981), there are, on the basis of distinctive culture, language, consciousness and political status, 73 ethnic groups in Europe. Said and Simmons (1976) estimate that in the world there are no less than 862 ethnic groups and, according to Connor (1971) only 12 of 132 independent states could be considered ethnically homogenous.

Within Britain there has long been a recognition of religious differences as well as of differences of language, dialect and culture between, for example, the Irish, Welsh, Scots, and Jews. What has happened is that post-war immigration from Europe, but especially from the New Commonwealth, has accentuated the pluralism of Britain. There has also been a worldwide trend of greater awareness of, and pride in (sometimes becoming fervent nationalism) one's own cultural identity and tradition. Indeed Banks (1981) argues that personal identity arises out of the interaction of ethnic, national and global identifications. In a society committed to liberty and equality, this implies a commitment to diversity, and all schools have a role in this process. Craft (1984) argues that in the interests of social cohesion children need help to acquire linguistic, cognitive and social skills of broader value, or they will be at a disadvantage. This is similar to Lynch's (1983) statement that 'curriculum content needs to embrace a core of common learnings related both to unity and diversity' (p. 70).

Many writers see this as the challenge of multicultural education, utilising the tensions produced in a creative and positive way. Sometimes, though, this is presented in a rather romantic light. There is no doubt that cultural diversity makes life interesting and produces creative tensions. These can be reflected and developed in the realms of literature, poetry, art, drama and film. However it also produces conflict of a threatening and destructive nature, which can seriously inhibit a person's life chances through the unchallenged growth of racist ideology and practices which must be confronted by schools.

SUMMARY

The criticism levelled at anti-racist multicultural education during the last few years has not been the sole preserve of its opponents. Much of the criticism has been internal, acknowledging that certain definitions and concepts lacked clarity, which impeded successful implementation at classroom level, as well as hindering the development of a coherent theoretical framework.

This has led to more succinct definitions of the aims and objectives of such a curriculum, but more importantly it has led to the development of guidelines for selection and evaluation. These are not presented as permanent, absolute or rigid criteria but are tentative and open to negotiation and refinement, particularly through experience of classroom practice.

Lack of clarity or coherence in anti-racist multicultural education is hardly an adequate base from which to call a halt to its implementation. When critics have pointed out the unresolved dilemmas of multi-cultural education, they imply that the notion of what 'education' is has been resolved and that there is a consensus of opinion which accepts this. In most comprehensives within Britain today there are competing definitions of 'education'. Firstly there is the idea that education is about acquiring directly relevant vocational skills. Anything which does not meet this requirement should either be deleted from a school's curriculum or seek to justify itself in vocational terms. Secondly there is the notion that education is about initiation into 'high culture' or the several forms of knowledge (such as the scientific, religious, aesthetic etc.) which serve to enlighten and civilise man. Finally education is seen as developing a child's potential through the provision of appropriate learning experiences relevant to the child and his or her ability and background. These conflicting, though not mutually exclusive, definitions can be seen at various levels in the education system, from the epistemology of some subjects to the pedagogical style of teaching or instruction, from the type of examination to the construction of a school's timetable, and whatever definition is dominant at the time will also be reflected in this way.

Consequently, to penalise anti-racist multicultural education for lack of cohesion in both its theory and practice is inappropriate, considering the practice of 'education' in schools today, and can be seen as an attempt to avoid the real issues raised by multicultural education. These issues of racism, cultural superiority, good practice, selection of curriculum content etc. are sometimes difficult to face and difficult to resolve. This is accepted by the advocates of anti-racist multicultural education, and attempts to resolve these difficulties and establish examples of good practice are well on the way. However, as Grant and Slater (1985) note, the implications of a full acceptance of diversity are considerable and may have yet to be fully appreciated by advocates of multicultural education they also note that 'the teacher directed textbook approach ... is probably not the appropriate teaching approach for the goals of multicultural education' (p. 111). Therefore teaching methods as well as content selection need greater attention if good practice is to be established.

The 1980s have been characterised by a kind of internal disagreement between 'anti-racists' and 'multiculturalists', which has resulted in greater clarity and attempts to bridge the gap as education enters phase six of its response to the multicultural nature of society. Criticism has also come from those who are not advocates of multicultural education, who see in the movement something much more sinister.

3

The new right: one Flew in the cuckoo's nest?

The educational response to Britain's increasing diversity has met with an increasingly hostile reaction in some circles, and since *Education for All* there have been a series of articles and books attacking Swann and LEA policies, especially as policies have spread beyond 'What the media complacently describe as the loony left' (Flew, 1987).

Multicultural and anti-racist education are perceived by Flew and others as a serious threat to education and society in general. For instance, Pearce (1986) sees multicultural education as undermining the native British way of life and it soon becomes apparent who is and is not to be regarded as native British. Flew though goes further and suggests that anti-racism has revolutionary intentions and is 'indoctrination in muddle and falsehood' (1986) because of Marxist-influenced definitions of the central concept of racism, which is structurally located in a historically exploitive society. Flew argues that the real intention of anti-racism and the 'race relations industry' is to 'conserve' the entire non-white population as an alienated and anti-British minority, ready to be recruited as storm troopers in the New Socialist cause' (1987). O'Keefe (1986) goes as far as to accuse those involved in the race relations 'lobby', such as the CRE, of promoting disharmony and causing riots, whilst anti-racists in teaching are totalitarian bigots, out to destroy democratic freedoms, through the appointment in some LEAs of what sections of the media referred to as 'race spies' or 'classroom commissars' as in Brent.

Lewis (1988) perhaps sums up what these writers argue should be the response to Britain's ethnic minorities when he states that they should not expect public institutions, such as the education system to take any steps to incorporate their customs, language or values. It is up to ethnic minorities to make the appropriate adjustments if they wish to benefit from British education.

One of the best-known critics of multicultural education is the former Bradford Headmaster, Ray Honeyford. His writings on the topic received wide-spread coverage during the 1980s in both academic and popular media, resulting in his acceptance of early retirement from his Headship of a multi-ethnic middle school. Halstead (1988) has provided the most authoritive and objective account of the events surrounding the writings of Honeyford, whose opinions on how the education system should respond to cultural diversity can be characterised as follows:

1 No concessions should be made to ethnic minorities in terms of dress, food, activities (e.g. PE) or curriculum content. Schools' role is to liberate children from the cultural constraints of the home background, the 'purdah mentality' (Honeyford, 1984). Any concessions are socially divisive as one group is seen to have special privileges, which leads to resentment.

2 Multicultural education is another product of progressive education which has undermined standards in many state schools and has become the latest 'fashionable bandwagon'.

3 It has no roots in British traditions or history, which render it a meaningless educational experience for children.

4 It has been imposed from above by 'official diktat' and does not have the support of most parents.

5 The acknowledgement that all cultures have equal validity will have profound consequences on schooling.

6 There is a hidden political agenda associated with multicultural education which is bent on radicalising pupils and changing society.

These criticisms have to be dealt with. They have, as noted by Oldman (1987), been couched in terms of 'plain speaking', decrying the trendy phrases and 'social science jargon' of many educationalists. As such, they have received considerable attention, especially from the popular press. It has to be born in mind that parents and many teachers in predominantly white areas are going to be influenced by the kind of arguments they are exposed to in the media, as their contact with the reality of classroom practice of anti-racist multi-cultural education is likely to be limited. This chapter addresses all of the issues raised by the severest of critics of anti-racist multicultural education.

Firstly, Flew argues that definitions of racism are frequently neglected in the literature or that the concept of racism is extended in some policy documents (e.g. those of ILEA and Berkshire) to institutional attitudes, modes of thinking and practices. What such policies result in is arguments in favour of positive discrimination or affirmative action which, according to Flew, (1986) translates as:

> If there are *n* percent of blacks and *m* percent of browns in the population as a whole then there will have to be *n* percent of blacks and *m* percent of browns in every profession, class, team, area or what have you. (p. 152)

There are two separate points here, the first of which, the lack of a definition of racism, shows a lack of thorough research, as virtually every writer has made an attempt to clarifty the concepts.

Flew reduces racism to the prejudiced behaviour of individuals and refuses to see 'race' as a social construct. Consequently, institutional racism not only does not exist but also is a 'repellent' concept. In the writings of these critics, race is usually seen solely in biological terms and is separate from any notion of culture. Racism becomes the 'odious' belief that 'one race is genetically superior to another' (Honeyford, 1986). Differences between groups can be explained by reference to these factors. Oldman (1987) points out how popular the biological explanation for behaviour has been through history at one time or another, accounting for madness, criminality and abnormal sexual behaviour, only to be discredited later. Such explanations do have a strong appeal in that they are simple and at the same time absolve others from any responsibility for unacceptable behaviour. In the case of race, the term has a long history as a scientifically valid concept, on which rested various racist ex- planations of humanity that have recently been revised (see Jones, 1986).

As Zec (1980) writes:

> No discussion of multicultural education at a philosophical level should seek to mask the unetched experience of many of our new settlers and their children of social and economic inequality rendered more damaging by racial prejudice and discrimination. (p. 29)

Flew's interpretation of any attempt at positive discrimination as resulting in some kind of quota representation is a gross exaggeration and misleading. Lynch (1986a) has dealt with this point in showing that any situation 'where everyone has to assimilate into fully mixed social, cultural and economic communities, ... would only be achieved by a level of directiveness and negation of freedom of choice, incompatible with democratic practice' (p. 11).

Indeed, many of the LEA policies as investigated by Troyna and Williams (1986) were opposed to positive discrimination. The emphasis has been on equalising opportunity. Policy statements' rather grand rhetoric tends to use the notion of 'perfect equality' as an ideal type construct to which education can contribute and not some kind of proportional equality 'imposed' by those in power.

Secondly, Flew argues that it is a mistake to assume that inequality of outcome is a result of inequality of opportunity, as there is evidence that cultural factors do effect educational achievement.

He (1987) castigates the Swann Committee for allegedly allowing itself to be intimidated by an internal minority with militant external support and abandoning any research on exploring the link between under-achievement and culture. For the report noted the differential achievement level between pupils of Afro-Caribbean, Chinese, Indian, Bangledeshi and Pakistani origin. What is neglected here is the reason why any ethnic group should feel misgivings about such research. The reason is bound up with a tradition of research which Mal Leicester (1989) refers to as the 'Pathology Syndrome', whereby for many years black disadvantage has been blamed on deficient black individuals, families or cultures. There has been little acknowledgement of the complex nature of the way racism operates, how it may take different forms with different ethnic groups, how age, gender and white expectations may interact to produce different reactions to racism. For Flew, though, and for others of the 'new right', cultural factors lie behind any under-achievement or inequality and not the way schooling is organised or delivered. Anti-racist multicultural education cannot form part of any solution to racial inequality because it is too political. The only research that is usually quoted in support of the ideas of the 'new right' is that of the American sociologist Thomas Sowell, who argues that the low socio-economic position in the USA of ethnic minorities is not due to racism or discrimination and that improvements can only be made through economic rather than political activity. However, as Rizvi (1989) points out, Sowell's analysis has been examined most recently by Boston (1988) and found to be wanting:

> Boston has argued that Sowell's analysis is biased because it does not include groups that have shunned political activity and have still remained economically and politically oppressed. Nor has Sowell established that some politically involved ethnic groups, such as the Jews, have not advanced economically. Moreover, it is ludicrous to maintain that American blacks would have been better off economically and socially had they not engaged in the Civil Rights movement.

Flew criticises those who attribute low ethnic minority achievement to 'hostile' discrimination within education, suggesting that the explanation for any under-achievement will be found in the culture and social patterns of the under-achieving group. However, most researchers agree that there is little overt 'hostile' discrimination on the part of teachers (see Jeffcoat, 1984a). What recent research does show is that what happens in classrooms can be very subtle discrimination based on teachers' ignorance, inexperience, hidden prejudice and differing expectations.

The Swann Report (1985) investigators 'ceased to be surprised when even in multiracial areas and schools, pupils and teachers refer to all non-white ethnic minorities collectively as 'Pakis' and their language as Indian or African' (p. 15).

Britain (1976) found that two-thirds of Heads had an unfavourable opinion of West Indian pupils and Tomlinson (1979) found that many Heads felt that the West Indian pupils' learning process was slower and they lacked concentration. Such a history of stereotypes of pupils and their abilities may not result in 'hostile' discrimination but in more subtle differential treatment based on differing expectations.

Research conducted by Green for the Swann Report (see Chapter 2, Annex B) on teachers' attitudes and pupil experiences in multiracial classrooms, concluded that:

> Boys and girls of different ethnic origins taught in the same multi-ethnic classroom by the same teacher are likely to receive widely different educational experiences, some elements of which may be differentially related to the teacher's gender, types of attitude held about education and when present extreme levels about education and when present extreme levels of ethnocentrism. (p. 53)

Cecile Wright (1985) attempted to put these experiences in the wider context of a pupil's school career. Her study focused on two secondary schools, one with 25 per cent ethnic minority and the other with 60 per cent. Most of these were West Indian. On entry to the two schools there was little or no difference between West Indian, white and Asian pupils in their reading ages, but the subjective comments from the junior school showed that the West Indians were perceived to be less co-operative.

During the first year, 33 per cent of West Indian pupils, in the school with 25 per cent ethnic minority pupils, were allocated to remedial groups, compared to 20 per cent white and 6.7 per cent Asian. At the other school, no white pupils were allocated to such groups. By the third year, the proportion of West Indians in the top bands and sets diminished significantly, serving to reduce option choices. By the end of five years secondary schooling, despite entering the schools on a par with white and Asian pupils, there was only one West Indian pupil in each school taking five or more O Levels. Wright's conclusion was that 'pupil–teacher relationships influenced teachers' professional judgement of pupils' ability and some West Indian pupils may have been placed in inappropriate ability groups and exam sets, so restricting their opportunities' (p. 22).

Eggleston's (1985) study of 600 pupils attending 23 comprehensive schools also concluded that 'both at and below sixth form level we found evidence that ethnic minority pupils may be placed on courses and entered for examinations at levels significantly below those appropriate for their abilities and ambitions' (p. 6).

In discussing under-achievement, Flew argues that the use of the term 'black' to cover Afro-Caribbeans and Asians is an attempt to conceal any differential educational achievement. He suggests that because differential achievement amongst ethnic minorities is a reality, then the major factor for any failure cannot be racism.

However, the differences in achievement between and within ethnic minority groups has been acknowledged. For instance, Rex (1986) comments that 'within each of these groups (Asians and West Indians) and within the sub-groups amongst them are numerous variations' (p. 209).

A review of research on under-achievement by Tomlinson (1986) revealed that despite evidence that Asians perform as well as whites and that both achieve higher than West Indians, this is not sufficient information from which to draw significant conclusions. For instance:

1 Tomlinson cites many studies which show that Asians achieve as well as whites, but only because they stay on longer in education.

2 Not all Asians achieve as well as whites, especially pupils of Bangladeshi origin. This was noted in the Swann Report and the Home Affairs Committee (1986) Report on Bangladeshis in Britain.

3 One study suggests that if social class is taken into account, Asians could be seen to be under-achieving.

4 In some studies West Indian pupils, especially girls, have been seen to achieve on a par with whites.

Consequently the relationship between ethnic group and achievement is not as clear cut once factors such as gender, class and country of origin and length of residence are taken into account, as well as the experience of schooling. All of this need not deny that cultural factors may explain some of the differences in levels of achievement. But to suggest that these differences have been concealed does an injustice to many writers in the field. A call for further research has often come from advocates of anti-racist multicultural education. Yates (1986) suggests that we should seek answers to why one racial group is more likely to be the victim of racial violence than another and the effect this has on schooling; do ethnic groups hold different images of education? How do these articulate with other aspects of a culture, its religion and family ties? How is education ranked as a source of status and prestige? It is this kind of research, along with classroom experiences and teacher expectations, which is now underway.

Flew's failure to consider the cumulative research findings on differential achievement and the ethnic experience of the process of education leads to a single factor explanation, reminiscent of the explanations offered to explain working class under-achievement. In other words, a 'blame the victim' notion of under-achievement, which is seen to be totally rooted in the victim's culture and life style: there is nothing wrong with the education system's procedures or practices. However this goes against the recent research findings of Green, Wright and Eggleston, who all call for further research to establish more clearly the origin of differential educational experiences, so that strategies can be developed to improve the situation and the professional skill of teachers, to the benefit of all children.

Thirdly, Flew objects to the view which he claims is propounded in the writings of multicultural and anti-racist educationalists that all cultures are equally valid. He argues that some cultures can be judged 'superior' or 'better' than others on the criteria of their developments in social practices, music, art, literature and language. What this leads to in practice, according to Flew, is that male-chauvinist, macho, racist cultures, when compared with sexually egalitarian, non-racist cultures, are to be deemed equally good.

Flew objects to the notion that you cannot have quality distinctions between cultures, a view which he claims was propagated by those originally trained or 'otherwise affected or infected by what is presented as social science' (1987, p. 121). His views on culture echo those of Scruton (1986) who argues that 'the moral law is universally valid and universally binding'. Therefore criteria for evaluating cultures, religion, morality, language, aesthetics, political institutions etc. are not constrained by cultural boundaries and British culture embodies these principles to a high order. Scruton argues that ethnic minorities should adopt British culture for these reasons and that it is all around them. British culture is, according to Scruton, a prime example of a secular culture which is 'open' and reaches out to others, and it has shown this by absorbing other cultural influences in its 'high' culture. 'Other cultures are at best educationally superfluous, and, at worst simply inferior' (Leicester, 1989). Scruton therefore argues that there is no case at all for multicultural education and that it would also fail to transit the common and high culture of Britain.

Flew (1987) argues that multicultural education for 'non white immigrants' (his term) means looking backwards rather than forwards into the culture and traditions of the nation they have chosen to join and assimilation is the only goal. Those for whom assimilation is unacceptable should not have come and for example, Bangladeshi should go back to Bangladesh. However, ethnic minorities could keep some of their own cultural traditions, such as language, through setting up their own organisations, but without any support from the State. Flew writes, 'it is preposterous and grotesque for state schools to try as some have done to teach such children what are supposed to be their native tongues. What are mothers' knees for if they are not to learn our mother tongues?' (1987, p. 123).

In using culture in the way he does, Flew's contrasting cultures are presented as homogeneous entities, and he implies that to accept one part of a culture is to accept everthing else. As pointed out, homogeneity of culture rarely exists in the world and there is no suggestion on the part of multiculturalists that critical judgement be suspended.

Flew suggests that developments in 'high culture' are the result of a superior language with which to deal with the concepts of truth and beauty. However, as Edwards (1974) points out, it may simply be that the use of language surrounding such concepts as truth and beauty makes them seem more logical and competent. In other words, it may be just a stylistic elaboration. Labov (1969) has shown that what was considered deprived and deficient speech has the same capacity for conceptual learning and the same logic as other forms of language. Flew's claim that anti-racists and multiculturalists see 'every language as equally good for every practical purpose' (p. 159) and that all cultures are equally good is not really born out by an examination of the writings on the subject.

However, Parekh's (1988) point is that all cultures are human creations and deserve respect. Multiculturalists are not saying that you cannot critically evaluate another culture but that to do so, it is necessary to understand that culture in its own terms. Any aesthetic judgements made within one culture are particular to that culture, but there is no universal or objective criteria to make judgements across cultures. Consequently some degree of relativism has to be accepted if knowledge is to be seen as tentative, uncertain and characterised by disagreement.

This is not to suggest that a curriculum based on these assumptions is easy to develop, for it is bound to be in tension and open to negotiation all the time, but it does make for a more stimulating and possibly more honest and truthful educational experience for all pupils.

Parekh acknowledges that the term 'multicultural' is perhaps a source of confusion, being seen as initiation into a variety of cultures, or as giving pupils bits of information about other cultures, or as cultural maintenance, all of which are suspect. How it differs from a monocultural approach will be dealt with in some detail later. For the moment it is sufficient to note that the accusations against multicultural education are without substance.

Another important point made by Parekh is that expecting ethnic minorities to disolve their identities through assimilation to an unchanged British culture is hardly the best expression of a liberal and tolerant culture. What Swann and others argue for is a redefinition of Britishness which takes full account of cultural diversity.

The fourth point made by flew is that one of the major drawbacks to the successful 'assimilation' of immigrants is the 'obsession' with racism. In the educational world this, Flew claims, leads to a campaign of 'political falsification and indoctrination' (p. 154) on the part of anti-racist multiculturalists. The alternative offered is 'to draw deep on the accumulated experience of a country which has in the last one hundred and fifty years accepted and assimilated the largest and most various immigration in the whole history of the world' (p. 160).

Learning aside, the hidden cultural superiority in the quotation, especially in the latter part, for Australia and the United States could make greater claim, raises the question: what exactly is this 'accumulated experience' and to whom is he referring? Flew's implication is that this experience has been the successful assimilation of various immigrant groups into an essentially tolerant and welcoming host society. However, the persecution of the Jews is a recurrent feature of British history. At the turn of the century, when Jews came to Britain fleeing from persecution in central Europe, they were met with suspicion and hostility from all sections of a society which feared for jobs, housing and schools from these 'strangers from abroad', as MP Evans Gordon put in in 1902.

Foot (1965) argues that during the 1930s, when Jews sought escape from Nazi Germany, Britain allowed some to enter but denied access to others because of a fear of antagonising anti-Semitic feeling in Britain if there was large scale Jewish immigration.

The influx of Irish people during the latter half of the last century may not have produced such hostility, but it is significant that both Irish and Jewish people tended to be confined to certain areas of cities and certain types of jobs. It is not so long ago that lodging houses carried the familiar 'No Irish' sign. Indeed the contempt in which many British (perhaps English would be more appropriate) hold the Irish is reflected in their continued low status in 'Irish jokes'.

Jones (1986) gives a detailed historical account of the presence and treatment of black people in Britain since Queen Elizabeth's proclamation forbidding the further settlement of 'blackamoors' within the city of London. The eighteenth century saw the development of the 'scientific' basis for racism from biologists such as

Long, who described African slaves in Jamaica as 'bestial, libidinous and shameless as monkeys and baboons' (quoted in Walvin, 1973). The philosopher Hume wrote: 'I am apt to suspect the Negroes and, in general, all the other species as men ... to be naturally inferior to whites' (quoted in Tierney, 1982).

The way in which such notions of superiority and inferiority enter into the cultural heritage of a society can be seen in an early edition of the *Encyclopaedia Britannica*, which described Afro-Caribbean people as full of 'idleness, treachery, revenge, cruelty, impudence, stealing, lying, profanity, debauchery, nastiness and intemperance' (quoted in Walvin, 1973, p. 175).

The contributions of Darwin, Spencer and Dalton all gave some academic and intellectual justification to notions of the hierarchical division of races, which placed whites at the top and blacks at the bottom. This was occurring at a time when Britain may have ended slave trading, but was coming into closer permanent contact with black people through colonisation.

Britain's colonies served her well economically and militarily, with significant involvement of colonical troops in both World Wars. For instance, by 1919, India had sent over one million men, along with troops from the West Indies, and suffered terrible casualties. However, despite appreciation in some circles, there were riots in Liverpool in 1917 when fifty black soldiers were attacked by 4–500 white soldiers. Further race riots followed in 1919 in Liverpool, Cardiff and Canning Town in London, resulting in random attacks on black people and the use of knives and revolvers (see GLC, 1986).

Palmer (1986) argues that there is little racial prejudice in Britain today and that what there is, is stirred up by the race relations industry. Unfortunately for Palmer this is an increasingly difficult position to maintain, considering the extent of the evidence that has accumulated over the past 25 years.

The three PSI studies of 1967, 1973/4 and 1984/5 revealed widespread discrimination in housing, employment and the provision of services. For instance, the 1973/4 study estimated that West Indians and Asians faced discrimination in 50 per cent of applications for unskilled jobs. A decade later it was found that the level of discrimination had not declined significantly. There is plenty of research evidence which reveals the extent of prejudiced attitudes (see Davey, 1983 and Milner, 1983) and discriminatory behaviour on the part of individuals and institutions (e.g. in medicine, the armed services, the police – see Smith and Gray, 1983).

Reference has already been made to research undertaken in education. Are the findings of the Swann Report, Green, Eggleston and Wright on the differential treatment given to black and Asian students on courses and in classrooms to be totally disregarded? If so, what about other evidence which has addressed the issue of racism? Research into racism in Norfolk's first and middle schools revealed the extent of racial harassment, name calling and bullying (Strohnach and Akhtar, 1986). In Glasgow, the Scottish Ethnic Minority Research Unit survey (1986) revealed that 100 per cent of respondents had been subjected to racial abuse and 37 per cent had experienced personal racial attacks. Research by Kelly and Cohen (1988), mainly in schools where the proportion of white English pupils varied from 50 to 66 per cent, revealed the extent of fighting and racial name calling which affected the Afro-Caribbean and Asian children as victims more than any other group. Carrington *et al.* (1987) showed that in an area where young South Asians made up 5 per cent of the population 'more than three-quarters of them were able to recount personal experiences of racism ranging from verbal abuse through to physical violence' (p. 83).

The CRE report, *Learning in Terror* (1988), documents cases of racial harassment and racial violence in Wales, the West Country, the North East and London. In addition, there is the evidence of the attitudes white pupils hold towards ethnic minorities, even though it may not always lead to violence or abuse. Win Mould's survey (1986) of 300 Tyneside children, ranging in age from 9 to sixth formers, found that 25 per cent held hostile attitudes but also that 75 per cent had negative attitudes towards black/Asian people, which was expressed in the form of crude stereotypes relating to employment, housing, social services, trouble and music. This pattern was also found during work at Frogmore Community school, Hampshire and the way it was used to heighten awareness within the school is the subject of Chapter 6.

Banks (1988) also notes that research in the USA has indicated that the values, goals and aspirations of, for example, Afro-Americans are strikingly similar to those of middle-class whites. This has often been commented upon by researchers in the UK, especially those concerned with young people. Although there are cultural differences between ethnic groups, these groups also share many cultural characteristics. Banks concludes that the cause of conflict between groups is 'racial rather than cultural'. This has significant implications for the type of educational programmes that are needed in our schools.

It is grossly insulting and intellectually dishonest to deny the existence, extent and effects of racism in Britain. All of the research conducted into these 'three Es' attempts not only to bring racism to light but also to suggest how the schools may best respond in terms of its curriculum and ethos. As Mould (1986) says:

> Keeping one's head in the sand may be more comfortable in the short term but in the long term there is no surer way to moral, social and educational disaster. (p. 12)

Of course, there are many individuals from ethnic minorities who have had favourable experiences in Britain, both today and in the past. However, at regular times we can see the anxiety that many people feel about Britain's increasing diversity surface. The reaction given to the possibility of large numbers of Hong Kong Chinese seeking entry to Britain with their 'alien culture' during the 1990s and the unwelcoming and suspicious reception accorded to Tamil and Kurdish refugees are examples.

Banks (1986) as usual tries to place educational developments into some kind of historical perspective and points out that a kind of neo-conservatism breaks out:

> when the groups that are trying to institutionalise pluralism begin to experience success and those who are committed to assimilation and to defending the status quo begin to fear that the pluralist reformers might institutionalise a new ideology and create new goals for the nation state. (p. 10)

Consequently, attacks such as those mounted by Flew, Scruton, Honeyford and Lewis have to be set in the wider context of a society going through a process of adjustment to the heightened diversity of the late twentiety century, which calls for a close examination of its education system: its procedures, values and content. How, in other words, to prepare all pupils appropriately for life in the twenty-first century?

The criticisms made of multicultural and anti-racist education are elitist arguments dressed as polemic and insult. This includes personal attacks on the Head of the CRE and others as well as on certain educational institutions. Flew goes so far as to suggest that teachers trained at the University of Keele and Goldsmith College should not be hired, because their training has included elements that could be described as anti-racist or multicultural.

The constant defence of the status quo in all areas of life eventually leads Lewis (1988) to call on ethnic minorities to stay out of politics, which is a very difficult proposition to justify in a supposedly open, tolerant and democratic society. The problem is that any challenge to the status quo, such as new political demands or an educational innovation, is seen as having ulterior and sinister motives invoking the 'spectre of indoctrination'. In reality, this is far removed from what happens in practice. For instance, two years into Brent's scheme to employ school-based co-ordinators for the authority's race equality programme (the notorious 'race spies' in the classroom), *The Sunday Times* (23 July 1989) reported that the scheme had won the approval of teachers, parents and governors. This has been achieved by the open and professional manner of many of the co-ordinators (race spies) who are part of the teaching staff and the community.

Some recent research on schooling is also instructive for those who are genuinely concerned with improvements in educational achieve-ment. Although the research by Smith and Tomlinson (1989) into inner city schools focused on differential achievement, they did comment that 'multicultural education policies have an inherent educational value' (p. 281). They also concluded that:

the measures that will best promote the interests of racial minorities in secondary schools are the same as those that will raise the standards of education generally. (p. 306)

The call for the abandonment of the kind of policies which assist in the above process, such as those of Berkshire and Hampshire, met with an interesting response when it was attempted in Berkshire. The authority received its biggest ever post-bag when its intention became known. Over 700 letters opposing the idea came from within and outside the county. They came from parents, teachers, Heads, lecturers, other professionals and representatives of the churches, easily dwarfing the handful of letters in favour. The policy stayed.

The frequent reference to Britain's traditional culture is never fully explained in the criticisms of anti-racist multicultural education. It is assumed that we know what it is. But just what is this apparently homogeneous culture? Does it include the Welsh, Scots and Irish? There are also other questions pertinent to the role of education.

From whose perspective is History taught? Does it include the variety of cultures and values found within Britain in the North, the South and the West Country, the urban/rural differences, the traditions and values of Chartism and socialism? Or is what is being referred to as British culture something a lot narrower and more authoritarian than this kind of cultural and intellectual diversity?

Anti-racist multiculturalism, on the other hand, does face up to these difficult issues and sees it as the responsibility of all schools. As Oldman (1987) points out:

> What is not remotely apprehended in the authoritarian writings is the idea of communities shaping their children's education in ways they feel to be valuable, even if this happens to contradict the traditions of existing curricula. (p. 42)

For those of us in mainly white schools, the question is whether we are to perpetuate the ignorance about ethnic minorities commented on by the Swann Report, whether we are to ignore the racism found in and out of schools, whether we are, in other words, prepared to condone and perpetuate the often racist mis-education of the majority.

DEMOGRAPHIC CHANGES

For those still unconvinced about the need to address issues of cultural diversity and racial equality in a positive manner, there are important changes taking place in the populations of many societies which will eventually force this to take place. Banks (1989) refers to this as the Demographic Imperative.

In the USA, for example, during the 1980s the gap between rich and poor has widened. By 1988, 10 per cent of whites, 30 per cent of Hispanics and 40 per cent of African Americans were living below the poverty line. Because the white population is aging and declining, while the population of 'people of color', especially Hispanics, is rising, 'people of color' will make up a disproportionate share of the work-force. Whites, on the other hand, will make up a disproportionate share of the retired population. In total, it is estimated that by the year 2000, people of color will make up a third of all Americans.

A recent report estimated that 'US colleges and Universities will have to graduate twice as many women, five times as many blacks and seven times as many Hispanics into Science and Engineering careers to fill expected shortages in the 21st century' (*The Times Educational Supplement*, 5 January 1990). As Banks (1989) says, 'America's poor children and children of color are its future'.

Consequently, there is a need for education to address the issue of inequality, under-achievement, discrimination and racism through anti-racist multicultural education. Indeed, the evidence from the USA indicates a substantial improvement in the performance of African Americans and Hispanics in Advance Placement examinations for Colleges, especially in schools with large minority enrolments.

In Britain, the proportion of 16–19 year olds will fall by one million between 1983 and 1993 (DES, 1988), and between 1988 and 1995 the number of 16–19 year olds in the British labour force will fall by nearly a quarter from 2.5 to 1.9 million. The proportion of school leavers who are from ethnic minority backgrounds will increase significantly, and the message already going out to employers is that they must examine their recruitment policies very carefully. As Michael Day put it: 'Employers in shortage areas who do not recruit from ethnic minorities may find they are unable to recruit at all' (1988).

It will not be just labour shortage areas to which this applies, but all sectors of the economy will be competing for a shrinking supply of labour.

There are already some signs that the achievement levels of most ethnic minorities has continued to rise over the last ten years, although by no means uniformly. With the plans to increase the numbers of students in higher education, there may well be real opportunities to reduce the extent of inequality in education and the labour market. However, as was stressed at the beginning of this book, the attitudes of the majority white population will remain largely untouched if anti-racist multicultural education is directed solely at improving the performance of ethnic minorities to meet temporary economic demands.

Britain, like the USA, is likely to enter a period of witnessing the translation of academic success amongst ethnic minorities into material and professional success on a much larger scale than before. What then is likely to be the social reaction to this situation without the provision of anti-racist multicultural education for all?

Perhaps a pertinent example is that of British Columbia in Canada. Here, there has been a small Chinese population for a hundred years, with a history of institutional discrimination which lasted until relatively recently. During the 1980s there was a deliberate and successful attempt to recruit entrepreneurs and investors from Hong Kong. The arrival of so many wealthy and talented Chinese has caused resentment and anxiety over such things as university places, professional jobs and house prices, as evidenced by these comments reported in the *Independent*, 17 January 1990:

> The Vancouver mainstream is having trouble coping with the fact that a Chinese can be more than a corner-store grocer ... If they see a Chinese family driving a Mercedes Benz, they think: 'That's despicable ...'

The fear is not that there will be an explosion of racial violence, but rather than the two communities will slide into mutual exclusiveness, from which it becomes very difficult to break out and upon which stereotypes and racism feed. It is exactly to this scenario that the 'new right' policies lead.

The only way in which situations like this can be avoided in any society is by all schools seeing anti-racist multicultural education as part of preparation for life in a rich, interdependent culturally diverse society: one which provides opportunities for the development of cross-cultural competencies and an opposition to all forms of racism, throughout all phases of the education system.

SUMMARY

Flew's argument is that to see racism as a structural, endemic phenomenon means to give in to the 'Marxist militants'. Racism is reduced to a natural condition of humanity, discrimination is underplayed and what failure exists educationally and economically is due to inherent genetic shortcomings or cultural deficiencies. However, to make a substantial case for these points necessitates a deliberate misrepresentation and distortion of the theory and practice of anti-racist multicultural education. This applies to the definitions of concepts, extent of under-achievement, views on culture and the historical development of racist ideas, and the relationship between different cultures within a colonial power. It is Flew's attacks on these and the alternatives proposed which, on close examination, are found wanting and appear motivated by political attitudes rather than intellectual concern. It amounts to a familiar message:

that in race, as in other things, the status quo must be upheld; that to attempt to challenge it can inspire only revolution and in such a message many may feel lies misery and despair. (Rose, 1987)

However it is important to place the development of anti-racist multicultural education and its critiques in a wider context, and perhaps to avoid some of the 'misery and despair' referred to by Rose.

Banks (1986) attempts a typology of ethnic revitalisation movements based on existing and emerging theory and research and ethnic events in the USA and UK. Banks argues that ethnic revitalisation movements are likely to pass through four main phases, which should be seen as dynamic and multi-dimensional rather than as static and unilinear.

Initially there is a pre-condition phase where there is a history of imperialism, colonialism and institutionalised racism. Victimised racial groups within a society are denied equality and justice despite democratic ideals, and when steps are taken by the State to improve the situation, this stimulates hopes and expectations. In the first phase, single-clause explanations and paradigms predominate with racism seen as the single causal explanation for inequality in jobs, education, health etc. Ethnic groups begin to forge a new identity for themselves by legitimising their histories and cultures with strong in-group feelings. A kind of ideological war breaks out between radical and liberal theorists while, at the same time, an anti-egalitarian ideology develops which sees the failue of ethnic groups as a result of inherited or family and cultural characteristics. Banks argues that the 1980's UK was like the USA in the 1960s and 1970s, as the phase is characterised not only by strong rhetoric but also by riots and rebellions. Banks argues that the situation remains stalemated until racism is acknowledged and steps are seen to be taken in an attempt to eliminate it.

The later stage is characterised by a search for multiple rather than single causes of inequality or under-achievement. Racism is seen as a legitimate explanation but only part of one, and because emotions cool there is more open discussion. Reforms are made by the State, both real and symbolic.

The final phase sees the institutionalisation of many of the reforms begun in the early and later phases. Reform movements broaden to include women and the handicapped, although this can create conflict in the competition for resources. This phase does not end until 'diverse ethnic and racial groups experience structural inclusion and equality within the nation state' (p. 9). However, Banks also argues that once such an ethnic revitalisation has occurred, then social, economic and political conditions tend to arise that give birth to new revivals. This cyclical process Banks suggests is beginning to happen in the USA.

According to Banks (1988) the UK is situated in the early ethnic revitalisation stage (perhaps it would be more accurate now to locate the UK at a slightly more advanced stage), which is comparable to the USA during the late sixties and early seventies. Consequently, the strong attacks on anti-racist multicultural education are to be expected at this stage. Banks also points out that 'educators who refuse to validate racism as an explanation or to take serious steps to eliminate it will extend the early phase of ethnic revitalisation' (p. 28).

Now that the anxieties and criticisms have been dealt with, if we are to progress in the way we educate our pupils for life in a multicultural society, we must continue to move towards the remaining phases of Banks' typology. One way is to make the case for the development of anti-racist education as good practice.

4

Anti-racist multicultural education in the new ERA

GOOD PRACTICE

There are several reasons for the slow growth of anti-racist multicultural education in all-white schools throughout the 1980s.

Firstly, there has been the media misrepresentation of this approach, which did not create a climate conducive to teachers and parents embracing such an apparently radical perspective.

Secondly, many all-white LEAs who developed policies were concerned to keep implementation at a low profile for political reasons and so only provided minimum staffing and funding.

Finally, there was the gap between rhetorical statements and the reality of the all-white context. How exactly was all of this relevant to their situation? Where were the examples of good practice? As Troyna and Selman (1989) noted, most of the examples quoted were drawn from inner city schools with significant numbers of ethnic minority pupils. (See, for example, Brandt, 1986.) Many advocates in their writing have assumed that teachers knew exactly what was meant by multicultural education and would need little convincing that it was a 'good thing'. This implied that at present schools were providing a narrow, racist curriculum. It is rather daunting and threatening for schools and teachers to accept such a proposition and then to attempt to address questions about the selection of knowledge, teaching styles, the hidden curriculum, school texts and the issue of truth and validity. As there was little pressure from local ethnic minorities in all-white areas for schools to do this, it could easily be given a low priority. As Page and Thomas (1984) point out, if all schools are to respond effectively in preparing pupils for life in a multicultural society, they have to be convinced on educational grounds.

One way of addressing this problem is to examine what passes for the curriculum in many of Britain's schools and to consider the effect it has on people's knowledge, understandung and attitudes towards other cultures and peoples. Parekh (1986) argues that 'the English educational system has a deep mono-cultural orientation' (p. 20) and points to several factors which contribute to this.

Religious education has concentrated heavily on Christianity, ignoring or only barely acknowledging the existence of other religions. Even if they are included they are frequently presented as 'primitive', 'fanciful', 'fanatical' or 'dogmatic'.

History has for many years, even before the National Curriculum, been the history of Britain, including wars with Europeans and development of the USA and lands of the Empire. The latter has usually been presented as having neither a culture nor a history before the arrival of Europeans. Those non-western civilisations included are judged by western cultural standards.

Geography has often been confined to Europe and America. The Third World has usually only been seen in terms of its problems, i.e. poverty, over-population and hunger, these being mainly due to the climate and ignorance of contraception and efficient farming techniques. Little attention is given to their social organisation or culture which would reveal that their behaviour 'made sense' in terms of local climate or habitat.

Sociology and Social Studies usually focus on Britain. What little cross-cultural work is done often presents such things as gender roles, marriage customs or the control of deviance as exotic or quaint.

English Literature in schools has been dominated by white English and American writers (often male as well). Many of these works have often perpetuated negative cultural stereotypes of Africans, Asians, Black Americans and Chinese. For example, the tradition of oriental villainy and decadence is a recurring theme in the writings of Dickens, Oscar Wilde, and the stories of Bulldog Drummond and the Fu-Manchu mysteries of Sax Rohmer (see Watson, *Snobbery with Violence: English Stories and their Audience* (1971) London: Methuen). Other cultures' Art, Music, Drama and Dance rarely feature in the Creative Arts curriculum in all-white schools.

The negative attitude and lack of proficiency of many British adults and children in relation to the learning and command of a foreign language has become legendary. As Parekh (1986) observes, 'An attitude to a language reflects an attitude to the people who speak it'.

Both the Science and the Mathematics curricula have ignored the history and contribution that non-European cultures and peoples have made in the development of scientific concepts, and even recent work by black scientists is ignored.

Such a curriculum (although only briefly outlined) would be recognisable to many who have passed through compulsory schooling during the past thirty years. Some of these individuals have gone on to become teachers or Head teachers, academics or administrators within education.

Previous chapters have already detailed the response of the education system to the presence of ethnic minorities and their culture, religion, language, dress and diet. The response, either direct or indirect in terms of policy, reflected the attitudes developed or reinforced through people's experience of a mono-cultural curriculum. The teaching of English was undoubtedly necessary, but was it necessary to devalue a child's mother-tongue? The insistence in many schools that a child's mother-tongue must never be spoken was taken without any evidence to support the notion that it would hinder educational progress. This, in fact, is contrary to recent findings of the positive effects of bilingualism. What attitudes lay behind the decision to advocate the 'bussing' of immigrant children rather than white?

Many Hindu children are vegetarian and Muslims do not eat pork. Muslim girls and some Hindus have a certain cultural tradition regarding undressing and wearing certain clothes for sports. However, many schools have shown little willingness to alter the school menu, tolerate alternative forms of sports attire or dress, exempt pupils from assembly or even give it a multi-faith flavour. This is because requests such as these have been interpreted by Heads or LEAs as pleas for special treatment. The argument put against such requests was that everyone was to be treated the same, which in practice meant that ethnic minority pupils should adopt white English customs and practices wherever possible.

If this has been the response of those who have had close contact with ethnic minorities and obviously represent an 'educated' stratum of society, what is the likelihood of those who do not have close contact with ethnic minority pupils or adults developing positive attitudes towards ethnic or cultural diversity? Much of the knowledge of these people will be formed by their experience in education and fed by media representation of ethnic minorities and the Third World, much of which is racist.

According to Parekh (1986), a mono-cultural curriculum results in:

1 A lack of curiosity about other societies and other cultures, as they are not exposed to them or, if they are, it is usually in a negative way.

2 A lack of imagination in conceiving of alternative ways of organising or resolving people's problems, encouraging 'the illusion that the limits of one's world are the limits of the world itself and the conventional way of doing things is the only way' (p. 23).

3 A stunting of the growth of critical faculties. This is because the child sees the world from the narrow perspective of his/her own culture and so rejects all that cannot be included in that. This leads to a judging of other cultures and societies by the norms and standards of one's own society. This can only result in admiring one's own greatness and genius.

4 A sense of arrogance and insensitivity. If other cultures and languages are not studied with sympathy and imagination, respect for them does not develop. It leads to a feeling of being threatened by diversity. Such an attitude is revealed in the way many English people expect, even when abroad, all 'foreigners' to speak English. Any attempts to learn or speak a foreign language, however tentative, are expected to be applauded enthusiastically, whereas 'foreigners' clumsy attempts to master English are the source of a long-established tradition in English humour.

5 A fertile ground for racism. This is because other cultures are judged by the pupils' own norms and values. This means that a pupil's 'home' culture is seen as a universally valid point of reference. Other peoples and their cultures will be evaluated in terms of their approximation to it. The closer they seem to be to one's own culture, the more civilised and developed they will be seen to be.

The manner and extent of this racism can be revealed through pupils' attitudes towards ethnic minorities. The views below were collected a few years ago in my own predominantly white school in a semi-rural part of north-east Hampshire. Pupils were asked to write anonymously on a variety of 'issues' of our time. These included football hooligans, abortion, ethnic minorities etc. They were encouraged to write their real feelings down, rather than what they thought teachers would like to hear. Various teachers participated in collecting these views. All had taught their classes over a lengthy period of time and knew them well. The writing of these views were, where possible, presented as a part of an ordinary lesson. In a school which encourages discussion skills, this was not difficult to do, even in Science lessons. What follows is a sample from the 25 per cent of pupils (all-white and mixed ability) who expressed particularly hostile views. They do not make for pleasant reading.

Fourth years

'West Indians are bloody horrible. I think they have taken over this country and they are a bunch of scums.'

'Paky's are smelly and I don't like them very much. They steal our jobs.'

'Pakistanis are black . . . and should be shot.'

'West Indians smell shit head.'

'Pakistanis are big bastards because they make a bloody mess.'

'West Indians – go to hell.'

'Pakistanis are scrounging bastards who don't deserve to be in Great Britain where they cause trouble (if they weren't here nobody could be Racist). West Indians are the same as Paks. But smell of curry.'

'Pakistanis are smelly because they don't wash their hair or use deodorant.'

First Years

On Pakistanis

'They aren't what I call lovely people. I don't know any and wouldn't want to. I don't understand why our country has got to have those Pakistanis in it. Soon there won't be enough room left for us English people and we'll end up moving out.'

'Don't like the way they talk and I don't like the way they do things.'

'Bud Buds.'

'Funny talking people.'

'I wish they would go home.'

'Should stay in their own country. A pain in the neck.'

On West Indians

'Don't smell very nice.'

'I don't like them.'

'Annoying, you find them everywhere.'

'They're food smells nasty.'

'Muhumbaganhdi.'

'I think they are wally's when they dance.'

'They seem dirty, the same as their surroundings.'

Fifth years

'I hate the Pakis because they are so dirty and they work all the hours that God sends and send all the bloody money back home to Grandma in the mud huts back in India.'

'I think that they should all leave the country, British born or not. They take all jobs what few we have. Most of them smell of B.O. and own shops.'

'West Indians. I don't know nothing about them but I don't like them. I haven't got any reason but that's my opinion.'

'Pakistanis are a pain in the arse.'

'They think that they are better than everybody else, they stink and they can't speak the English language properly. I say get rid of them.'

'They smell, they can't talk properly and lots of curry shops pop up from nowhere.'

Third Years

The following examples reveal how pupils, by the third year, have picked up sufficient messages to verbalise their 'correct' opposition to discrimination, while still hanging on to their prejudices. The comments opposite each other are from the same pupil.

On race and discrimination
'I think it's not fair to judge people by their colour. Racial

On immigration
'As long as they have *good* reason. Some of the laws are a bit

discrimination is unfair and employers should give Blacks more of a chance instead of thinking of them as an outsider who doesn't belong in this country.'

'I think that black people shouldn't be put down by their colour and should get a fair job or be judged as equals. Bias in books is bad and teaches young children prejudice. Calling black people names like wog is wrong because it can be very offensive.'

'It doesn't really bother me. I've got nothing against anyone from other countries.'

'I think that black people get all the rotten jobs because of the bias of white employers. And I think they should be treated the same as white people.'

harsh. Though they need to be, else we would turn into a country full of blacks and people of different race!'

'I think they should stay in their own country because each time someone comes here they are pushing our unemployed up and not helping Britain one bit. You can't go into London without seeing a black person. I think they are taking over Britain.'

'I don't think that black people have the right to live here as much as we do.'

'I think that Pakis, Black people and Chinese people should not be allowed to Britain. Because some people in Britain need houses more than foreigners. They should go back to their own country.'

Not all views were as hostile as these examples but, on average, the percentage expressing negative views was between 50 per cent and 75 per cent. This was even the case in classes in the fourth year, which had been through a unit of work on 'Race' that explained reasons for immigration and attempted to dispel popular myths about ethnic minorities, giving a more positive image.

These results are very similar to those found by Win Mould (1986) in a similar but larger survey of 320 children on Tyneside. Here again, their writings revealed that 75 per cent held negative attitudes towards black and Asian people and about 25 per cent of these held strongly hostile attitudes. The Swann Report (1985) commissioned research on the curriculum and pupil attitudes in 26 schools with few or no ethnic minority pupils (see Annexes C and D of Chapter 5). The report concluded:

> The project revealed widespread evidence of racism ... ranging from unintentional racism and patronising and stereotyped ideas about ethnic minority groups combined with an appalling ignorance of their cultural backgrounds and life styles and of the facts of race and immigration, to extremes of overt racial hatred and National Front-style attitudes. Asian pupils, usually viewed collectively as 'Pakis' seemed to be most frequently the object of animosity, dislike and hatred, apparently because of their greater perceived 'strangeness' and 'difference' from the accepted cultural, religious and linguistic norms. (p. 234)

Such attitudes were confirmed by Cochrane's and Billig's survey (1984), already referred to, in which they describe the prevalence of a kind of 'genteel fascism' distinct from the overt racism sometimes associated with sections of the white working class. A survey for *New Society* (1986) revealed 42 per cent of young people admitting to some degree of prejudice against other races and referred to the alarming growth of racial prejudice.

The extent of racism in British society is undoubtedly considerable, but as well as finding it repugnant we have to remember, as Carlton Duncan (1986) points out, that some of 'these youngsters later became teenagers – who then go out to perpetuate the kind of myths, preconceptions and stereotypes' (p. 66). For not only does the white ethnocentric school curriculum not challenge such attitudes, nor does what passes for teacher training do so.

Thus there is a strong moral argument for a more multicultural and anti-racist curriculum, but it needs to be accompanied by an equally strong educational argument in order to convince the many doubters over education's right or role to build or challenge certain attitudes. The recommendations of Swann do give some legitimacy to this process, acknowledging the need to 'change attitudes amongst the white majority' (p. 269) and stating that all schools need to respond to cultural diversity through major curriculum reviews and change.

What follows is an attempt to outline briefly the nature of an anti-racist multicultural curriculum in an all-white school, which not only serves to combat racism but enriches the traditional school curriculum and can be justified on educational grounds.

THE NEW ERA AND THE NATIONAL CURRICULUM

Since the Swann Report there have been several publications offering guidance on practical opportunities for curriculum developments along anti-racist multicultural lines, such as Craft and Klein (1986). Suitable materials have also been produced by teachers in LEAs which have set up support services to assist in the implementation of a county policy. By now they cover all curriculum areas from Science and Technology to Arts and Humanities. The best way to get in touch with these materials is through Access to Information on Multicultural Education Resources (AIMER), which supplies a comprehensive print-out of materials with details of age ranges and cost. There are also materials from mainstream publishers who have begun to respond to the criticisms made by teachers and parents about the ethnocentric or racist nature of many fiction and non-fiction books. In addition to these developments, charities and other organisations as diverse as Oxfam, the Intermediate Technology Group and the British Film Institute have begun to produce educational materials for use in all types of schools and colleges.

What this means in practice is that teachers who previously voiced the view that they would like to do something about the nature of their curriculum but there were not the resources to support this, no longer have this as a valid excuse, even in all-white contexts. Of course, resources aren't always the key to countering racism and stereotyping. How they are used in the classroom is all important and I shall return to the question of pedagogy later.

The major developments of the late 1980s with far-reaching consequences have been the Education Reform Act and the National Curriculum. The culmination, according to Ball and Troyna (1989), of a process which began with the Great Debate in the mid 1970s, when under a Labour Government there was concern about standards, teachers, curriculum content and vocationalism in education, and which continued in the 1980s with renewed vigour under the Conservatives, especially from 1987 onwards.

At first many believed that concepts such as cultural diversity, multiculturalism and anti-racism would disappear completely from the educational agenda given the Government's ideological position. However this did not happen once political rhetoric had to be translated into educational practice.

The DES *Circular 5/89, The Education Reform Act 1988: The*

School Curriculum and Assessment, states in sections 16 and 17 the aims of the school curriculum.

16. Section 1 of the Act, which came into force on Royal Assent, states the aims of the curriculum as a whole and places them in the context of the needs of pupils and society. It says that the curriculum should be balanced and broadly based, and should:

'a) promote the spiritual, moral, cultural, mental and physical development of pupils at the school and of society; and

b) prepare such pupils for the opportunities, responsibilities and experiences of adult life.'

17. This restates and extends the list of central purposes for the curriculum in Section 7 of the 1944 Act; in particular, it emphasises the need for breadth and balance in what pupils study, and that cultural development and the development of society should be promoted. It is intended that the curriculum should reflect the culturally diverse society to which pupils belong and of which they will become adult members. It should benefit them as they grow in maturity and help to prepare them for adult life and experience – home life and parenthood; responsibilities as a citizen towards the community and society nationally and internationally; enterprise, employment and other work. The requirements of Section 1 apply to *all* pupils – regardless of age – registered at *all* maintained schools, including grant-maintained schools, except that they do not apply to pupils in nursery schools or nursery classes in primary schools.

The National Curriculum Council set up to oversee the introduction of the National Curriculum states in its remit that: 'It will be taking account of ethnic and cultural diversity and ensuring that the curriculum provides equal opportunities for all pupils regardless of ethnic origin or gender' (NCC, 1988).

All Subject Working Groups have had cultural diversity as part of their brief and it is worth looking at some of the statements produced so far.

The English document, although not above pertinent criticism, does state:

2.8 A major assumption which we make is that the curriculum for all pupils should include informed discussion of the multi-cultural nature of British society, whether or not the individual school is

culturally mixed. It is essential that the development of competence in spoken and written Standard English is sensitive to the
knowledge of other languages which many children have. As
well as the many different mother tongues that are present in our
multi-cultural, multilingual society, there are also the foreign
languages that are taught in schools. A rich source of insight into
the nature of language is lost if English is treated in complete
isolation.

7.5 Today, literature in English in the classroom can – and should –
be drawn from different countries. All pupils need to be aware
of the richness of experience offered by such writing, so that they
may be introduced to the ideas and feelings of cultures different
from their own. English teachers should seek opportunities to
exploit the multicultural aspects of literature. Novels from India
or Caribbean poetry might be used for study of differing cultural
perspectives, for example. Not only should this lead to a
broader awareness of a greater range of human 'thought and
feeling', but – through looking at literature from different parts
of the world and written from different points of view – pupils
should also be in a position to gain a better understanding of the
cultural heritage of English literature itself.

The Science document is also quite explicit:

7.12 Science education must take account of the ethnic and cultural
diversity that the school population and society at large offers.

7.16 More generally, the science curriculum must provide opportunities to help all pupils recognise that no one culture has a
monopoly of scientific achievement – for example, through
discussion of the origins and growth of chemistry from ancient
Egypt and Greece to Islamic, Byzantine and European cultures,
and parallel developments in China and India. It is important,
therefore, that science books and other learning material should
include examples of people from ethnic minority groups
working alongside others and achieving success in scientific
work. Pupils should come to realise that the international
currency of Science is an important force for overcoming racial
prejudice.

For many years those involved in Design and Technology have
endeavoured to remain non participants in the debate on an anti-

racist multicultural curriculum relying tenuously on the 'technology is neutral' argument. The 5–16 document on Design and Technology states:

1.46 It is important that teachers take a positive approach to a mixed range of cultural backgrounds in their pupils, rather than an approach which concentrates on the problems that some pupils have in coping with, for example, the language of design and technology. The variety of cultural backgrounds of pupils can broaden the insight they all have into the range of appropriate, alternative solutions to perceived problems. There are rich opportunities here to demonstrate that no one culture has a monopoly of achievements in design and technology. Appreciations of this kind could both contribute to better international understanding and yield direct economic benefits in later life. It is equally important that schools where there are few or no ethnic minority pupils ensure that their pupils understand the cultural diversity of modern society and are aware of the diversity existing in areas in which they may later live or work. Design and technology, like other subjects in the curriculum, has an important part to play in preparing pupils for life in a multicultural society.

There are many valid criticisms of the *History Final Report* in terms of the selection of content and development of skills. However, the final report of the History Working group explicitly recognises the past and present cultural diversity of Britain and sees a major contribution of History to be the imparting of knowledge of the diversity of cultures within Britain and the development of skills which 'assist in identifying, and thus combating, racial and other forms of prejudice and stereotypical thinking' (11.26). This is also included in the stated expectation, considering the political pressure surrounding the drafting of the document, and it is far more than others wanted.

The History document does place British History at the core of the 5–16 curriculum, although the report does state that 'that does not mean that it is, or has to be, pivotal' (4.26). However, most of the Core History Units do focus on Britain. But in this there may be opportunities for sound anti-racist multicultural approaches. For example in Key Stage 2, Units on 'Victorian Britain', Life in Britain since 1930' and 'Exploration and Encounters' can be permeated with this perspective and there are resources available which can assist in this process. Optional Units such as 'Food and Farming' and 'Houses and Places of Worship' also lend themselves to this approach. (For examples of curriculum ideas, see Hix Wheatons, forthcoming.) The School Designed History Units offer the opportunity to develop local history schemes of work. There is no reason why such work could not be shared with other schools: for example, between multi-ethnic and all-white schools through school twinning arrangements, exploring internal and external migration, sacred places and the experience of racism and discrimination. This could involve visits and exchanges or incorporate the use of IT and electronic mailing, whereby pupils exchange information about their areas either on a national or international basis.

At Key Stage 3, 'Expansion, Trade and Industry' does allow for the development of work on the slave trade and the Empire, which is, of course, central to any anti-racist multicultural work, and there are now suitable materials to accomplish this task. This would also apply to the Optional Unit on 'Black Peoples of the Americas: C16th to early C20th'.

Consequently, there are opportunities for the maintenance and development of anti-racist multicultural approaches throughout the 5–16 curriculum in terms of specific units of work and the encouragement of cross-curricular approaches.

Another document this time from the DES, *National Curriculum: From Policy into Practice* (1989a), is notable for the explicit reference for the first time to multicultural issues:

3.8 The foundation subjects are certainly *not* a complete curriculum; they are necessary but not sufficient to ensure a curriculum which meets the purposes and covers the elements identified by HMI and others. In particular, they will cover fully the acquisition of certain key cross-curricular competences: literacy, numeracy and information technology skills. More will, however, be needed to secure the kind of curriculum required by section 1 of the ERA (see paragraphs 2.1-2.2). The *whole* curriculum for *all* pupils will certainly need to include at appropriate (and in some cases all) stages:

- careers education and guidance;

- health education;

- other aspects of personal and social education; and

- coverage across the curriculum of gender and multicultural issues.

These areas of the curriculum are not separately identified as part of the statutory National Curriculum because all the requirements associated with foundation subjects could not appropiately be applied to them in all respects. But they are clearly required in the curriculum which all pupils are entitled to by virtue of section 1 of the Act.

This distinction between the basic curriculum of core and foundation subjects and the whole curriculum is of central concern in the development of anti-racist multicultural education. In 'The Whole Curriculum' (1990) the NCC spells out more clearly this aspect of the curriculum. It distinguishes between cross-curricular Themes, Dimensions and Skills. Dimensions include a commitment to equal opportunities and 'a recognition that preparation for life in a multicultural society is relevant to all pupils and should permeate every aspect of the curriculum.' Included in Themes are Economic and Industrial Understanding, Careers, Health and Environmental Education, and Education for Citizenship. All of these lend themselves to an anti-racist multicultural perspective, especially Education for Citizenship which includes, as part of a suggested framework for schools, reference to the notion of the benefits of living in a plural society and human rights. In implementing all of this, the NCC suggests that all schools undertake a curriculum audit and produce whole curriculum development plans. As part of this review the school should examine its policies on such aspects as PSE, equal opportunities, special needs, assessment and multicultural education. One of the underlying assumptions here is that, if there is not a policy, then there should be! Indeed, the document goes on; 'Schools have or should have agreed policies and practices on cross-curricular dimensions', and:

The ethos of the school should support the school policy on equality of opportunity by countering stereotypes and prejudice, reducing the effects of discrimination and helping pupils to accept social diversity.

This aspect of the curriculum will need some form of INSET to take place in many all-white schools, and what follows in Chapter 6 may be of some assistance to schools in planning their implementation of this requirement.

The emphasis now placed by the NCC on these Dimensions permeating the whole curriculum may provide the opportunity for links to be made between race, class and gender, as 'the curriculum must aim to meet the needs of all pupils regardless of physical, sensory, intellectual, emotional, behavioural difficulties, gender, social and cultural background, religion or ethnic origins.

One example of how a topic or theme can be referenced to the National Curriculum and attainment targets is given in Figure 1. This is taken from *Primary School Links: An Approach to Education in a Multicultural Society* (P. Hix Wheatons, forthcoming). Here a popular theme of 'Communication' is approached from an anti-racist multicultural perspective, with its carefully specified objectives all related to National Curriculum requirements. Each particular activity directed at achieveing these objectives can be referenced in a similar way. It also gives an indication to secondary schools of how they may begin to plan for the incorporation of cross-curricular themes and how subjects can 'contract out' the assessment of some of their attainment targets to this aspect of the curriculum.

Although there have been these encouraging developments, they have not been enthusiastically welcomed by some supporters of multicultural and anti-racist education and have provoked con- siderable debate on the way forward for such approaches.

CURRENT CONCERNS AND THE WAY FORWARD

The concern relates to the wider context and manner in which the changes in education are taking place as well as the possible consequences of LMS and opting out. This has led to a debate about future strategy for those involved in anti-racist multicultural education and about how much involvement there should be with some of these changes.

There is a feeling among many educationalists, which is expressed by Grinter (1989), that change is taking place for economic and political reasons rather than for educational reasons and that National Curriculum developments involve a narrow definition of British society: for example, the emphasis on a broadly Christian Religious Education syllabus and acts of worship, the narrow History guidelines

Activity	English	Maths	Science	D&T	History	Geography	Music	PE (Dance)	Art	RE
1	3 Media					6				
2	1 2 3 Media		14	IT/12		2 7				
3	2 3									
4	1 2 Media									
5	1 Media					2 3 4 6 8				
6	2 3 Media				2 4					
7	1 2 Media				2					
8	1 Media									
9	1 2 3					6				
10	1 2 3 Media					6				
11	1 2 3				1 2 3 4					
12	1 2 3					6				
13	2 3									
14					1 3 4	6				
15	2								*	*
16	3									
17	1	A1/F1			1 3	6				
18	1 Media		1 6 12 14	1 2						
19			12 14	4 IT/1–5						
20	1 2 3									
21				2					*	
22							*	*		

Figure 1 *Attainment targets for 'Communication' theme*

which Grinter refers to as 'an invitation to ethnocentricism', and the resistence to the inclusion of community languages in the Modern Languages curriculum. This will obviously work against the much wider perspectives so fundamental to anti-racist multicultural developments. Reehana Minhas (1988) expresses the fears of many when she refers to the National Curriculum as a 'nationalistic curriculum', especially because of its emphasis on British history. She also points out that very few black and Asian organisations received consultative documents and that those that did, such as the West Indian Standing Conference and Afro-Caribbean Education Resource Centre (ACER), referred to them as a charter for racism. Many black and Asian colleagues and parents still have not had these fears allayed.

The wider context is, according to Minhas, the other Government changes which are directed at reducing the power of local authorities, though housing and welfare policies and the poll tax. The effect of the latter may effect the education service adversely if attempts to keep the tax down result in job losses. One example of that has been the abolition of Ealing's highly regarded Race Equality Unit, due to the change in political control in the borough. The growth in the central control and direction of the education service is according to Minhas (1988), creating an authoritarian state, and the National Curriculum is 'an authoritarian attempt to prescribe state schooling in order to churn out subserviant uncritical pupils – tomorrow's workers' (p. 9).

The racist implications of the Education Reform Act have been confirmed with ratification of the decision of Cleveland Education Authority to allow a parent to exercise choice on racist grounds. This precedent which establishes the primacy of recent Education legislation over Race Relations legislation opens the way for the growth in educational apartheid which is a trend with considerable implications for race-equality programmes. This may be compounded with open enrolment leading to popular academic schools being populated by mainly white middle-class pupils as a consequence of the publications of school examination results. The fear is that a school, its pupils and their parents become trapped in what Hatcher (1989) refers to as 'a spiral of decline' as the school begins to lose out in attracting pupils with a wide range of abilities, adequate resources and adequate staffing. Minhas (1989) and others argue that in practice this will amount to the reintroduction of 'secondary moderns by the back door' with schools segregated from each other by class and race, with further demarcations around those that opt out of LEA control.

Of immediate concern to all schools is the effect of the delegation of financial control to the school under LMS, especially the formula used to establish the size of its budget. Examples so far published in the educational press have resulted in the creation of a new educational phrase: 'formula-induced underfunding'. This is because the formulas used by LEAs to establish school budgets seem to result in a redistribution of resources away from inner city schools and those with experienced, high-cost staffs. Many such primary schools report facing budget shortfalls of between 8 and 15 per cent. As Minhas (1989) points out:

> Demographic patterns of settlement are determined by socio-economic and political factors. The majority of inner city communities are working class and a substantial number are black and other ethnic minorities. (p. 18)

The consequence for the quality of education in such schools for all pupils is rather obvious and will only serve to further segregate pupils and their communities. Vigilance and joint campaigns by teachers and parents are going to be needed in order to offset the possible gross inequalities of the effects of LMS.

Grinter (1989) implies that, because anti-racist multicultural education is not happening in those areas where it should, i.e. suburbia, under LMS there is now even less likelihood of any developments, as it will not be seen as one of a school's priorities. However, according to Carrington and Short (1989b) one of the reasons for this lies with the anti-racist movements itself which has failed:

> to provide unambiguous and workable strategies for implementation and to take account of variation in pupil responses according to their age and ethnic composition of their school. (p. 232)

How to overcome this is part of the rationale of this book and is now being addressed by other writers.

Hatcher (1989) and Minhas (1989) have both drawn attention to the effects of the changed relationship between schools and LEAs under LMS. Hatcher poses the question of what kind of support services the LEA can provide with the 10 per cent of funding which it can retain. This will gradually reduce to 7.5 per cent. For example, prior to LMS, Hampshire had 240 Advisory Teachers. Now it can budget for fewer than 100. The effect of this on the range and depth of education are significant. Minhas points out that many of those LEAs which have equal opportunities policies have also developed differential resourcing, dependent on school and pupil needs. Special curriculum projects have been set up to tackle the kind of issues dealt with in this book, such as curriculum content, overt and covert racism and managing change at personal and institutional levels. These projects have not always been confined to multi-ethnic areas, as post-Swann projects run from the Grampians to Cornwall. The concern is that LMS will curtail or marginalise these projects, rather than build on the examples of good practice being developed, especially in all-white areas.

It is quite obvious that those involved in the field of anti-racist multicultural education are alert to the possible negative effects of all the recent and proposed changes in education. Therefore strategies have to be devised which will turn the current culture and discourse of education to the advantage of anti-racist multicultural education.

One strategy offered by Gill (1989) is to ensure that the developing use of school performance indicators as a major tool of evaluation of school effectiveness includes criteria relevant to anti-racist multicultural principles. It has already been recognised that raw examination results are not in themselves a reliable guide to the effectiveness of a school. Other areas for which performance indicators may be developed would include:

Management of staff;

Management of curriculum and programmes of study;

Pastoral management;

Liaison with other agencies and the community.

What Gill argues for is the building of race equality issues into these and other indicators, so that the school's relationship with LEA and national policies relating to anti-racist multicultural education can form one assessment indicator. The same could apply to ethnic minoriting, levels of achievement, preparation for life in a multi-cultural society, contact with parents, and school policies. As Gill states:

The success criteria for all performance indicators should include race equality dimensions wherever these can be made to relate to the school's pupil intake. (p. 12)

Those best placed to assist schools in this process are LEA Inspectors along with Heads, teachers and parents. The concept of 'an effective school' in a multicultural society can be explored, as can the ways that this can be evaluated through inspection. LEAs which have developed policies and examples of good practices are in a better position to do this, and it is up to Inspectors and teacher colleagues to ensure that success indicators are developed relevant to anti-racist multicultural education.

Through prudent use of the mandatory exceptions under LMS, LEAs will still have as part of their support services Teacher Advisers. Some of these will have a wide equal opportunities or anti-racist brief, or perhaps a curriculum development role. However, with LEA Inspectors spending about 50 per cent of their time on inspection, these Teacher Advisers have an important INSET role to play in the early years of LMS, performance indicators and the National Curriculum. This will be within both subject specific and cross-curricular areas to ensure that the references to cultural diversity and combating racial prejudice are a feature of staff training and programmes of study.

Anderson (1989) argues that because there are opportunities in the National Curriculun they must be taken and used to spread the examples of good practice which already exist. Anderson points out that those teachers who have been practising anti-racist and multicultural approaches over the last few years are not suddenly going to abandon them. (For Anderson, anti-racism is just a part of good multicultural education.) One example of this is an account of two infant teachers (*Issues in Race and Education*, 58, Autumn 1989) which was appropriately titled 'Shaping It to our Purpose'. Here they described their water project and how it incorporated anti-racist multicultural approaches and met attainment targets in Mathematics and Design and Technology. However, one factor which might have some bearing on these developments is that not only the content of some National Curriculum subjects (e.g. History) but also the method of assessment may constrain teachers to the familiar and parochial, as well as didactic, teaching style.

For Eggleston (1988), however, testing offers a real prospect of benefit for black and Asian children. In his report, *Education for*

Some (1986), it was documented how teachers very commonly underestimated the achievements of Afro-Caribbean and Asian pupils. As Hatcher (1989) remarks:

> Some black parents have welcomed the national curriculum and national testing as a guarantee that their children will not be fobbed off with a second rate curriculum or suffer discriminatory subjective assessments by prejudiced teachers. Others have seized on the possibilities of LMS for ensuring that black people's voices can no longer be disregarded by the schools. (p. 24)

With ethnic monitoring, this should have an effect on all schools and their pupils, regardless of the actual number of ethnic minority students in the school.

Smith (1989) points out that the real opportunities for anti-racist multiculturalism lie in the space between policy and classroom practice. Even if teachers have to concentrate mainly on British history, contact with other countries cannot be avoided within that curriculum and the consequences which followed from the manner of that contact. Black and Asian contributions to Britain's own history can still be included as well as contributions to art and science. The cross-curricular approaches encouraged by the NCC may be more suited to issue-based and experiential modes of learning, which may be very effective in delivering an anti-racist multicultural perspective. For instance, Migration is a very popular upper junior and lower secondary topic, which can incorporate elements of both History and Geography in an anti-racist multicultural perspective.

All cultures express themselves through the visual and performing arts. An Arts curriculum for a multicultural society in any school should be enriching, extending all pupils' experiences, familiarising them with art forms created and valued by different cultures. A tokenist approach has to be avoided, i.e. that which sees non-western art forms as exotic or primitive.

Drama can be used to explore issues relating to prejudice, labelling and racism with all pupils in a variety of ways. In addition, there are also Theatre In Education groups whose members are drawn from ethnic minorities and who will address race relations issues directly with 'all-white' pupils.

There is a considerable amount of Music that pupils need to be aware is 'borrowed' from other cultures, especially in the area of popular music. The origins and development of this can offer an immediate and relevant contribution to inter-cultural understanding. This multicultural perspective can be extended by basing Music teaching on composition and performance which combines examples from different cultures, showing there are many ways of making and enjoying music.

Grinter (1989) makes it quite clear that in his view 'It is essential to work with and through the National Curriculum: there is no alternative' (p. 35). He goes on to identify six guiding principles to ensure the continuing development of anti-racist and multicultural perspectives. These principles sum up much of the above, emphasising:

The link to examples of good practice;

Identifying and challenging stereotyped views and assessments;

Permeation of the whole curriculum through global perspectives;

Teaching and learning methodologies which combat racism;

Learning related to student experiences;

Cross-curricular thematic work.

For these principles to be translated into action, Grinter acknowledges, is dependent on the commitment of groups of educationalists and parents, who will be working in a climate which will not always be favourable. This may especially apply to all-white areas, where an anti-racist multicultural curriculum has to earn its place. It can only do so by working with and through the National Curriculum and other educational developments, such as performance indicators. It has to show teachers and parents that it is 'predicted on democratic values', directed towards moral and political autonomy.

Unfortunately, however, much of the current debate has fallen into what Leicester (1986) refers to as the 'either/or' fallacy. When the term was originally used, Leicester was referring to the attacks made on anti-racist multicultural education by Flew and others. Their emphasis on the paramountcy of Standard English, as anything else would be detrimental to the child, is an example. Leicester pointed out that because people need to master Standard English, it does not follow that there is no educational merit in mastering Urdu or Creole. Both are perfectly valid educationally in a culturally diverse society.

This either/or fallacy has also characterised much of the discussion regarding the appropriate reactions to the new ERA changes. Basically, the choice has been seen as either joining in with the changes or having nothing to do with them and fighting outside the system. This restriction of possible reactions to a new education climate is rather similar to that criticised by Leicester and represents a cognitive style rather too easily equated with the results of a mono-cultural education deeply rooted in English culture, in terms of content and pedagogical style. (See Tomlinson, 1989 for details of the origin of the ethnocentric curriculum.)

Reference was made earlier to the criticisms of the mono-curriculum by Parekh (1986). One of the points he has made several times is the way such a curriculum fails to develop an individual's imagination. By this he does not mean aesthetic imagination, which might involve vivid impressions, sensual images, emotions or fantasy, but rather sympathetic imagination. This is the ability to 'rise above one's own values, preferences and views of the world ... and appreciate modes of thought and behaviour that might be profoundly different from one's own and even repulsive' (1986, pp. 86–7). An example of this is the well-documented reluctance of the British to learn another language, which would give greater insights into others, and the tendency to anglicise foreign-sounding names. Perhaps this lack of sympathetic imagination is best demonstrated by the reaction of many of those charged with the running of the education system to the presence of ethnic minorities in British schools particularly, in the way that they:

> cannot understand why anyone should be different, why everyone cannot eat the same food, dress the same way, hold the same ideas of propriety and modesty, speak the same language. (p. 21)

What has to be borne in mind is that this reaction is not confined to those who left school at an early age but has come from those who passed through further and higher education to attain positions of power and influence.

It is a mono-cultural curriculum which fails to develop a sympathetic imagination and hinders our ability to understand and respect others or to conceive of alternatives in human behaviour. Such a curriculum traditionally ignored diversity and devalued alternative perspectives (if any were presented), in sharp contrast to an anti-racist multicultural curriculum where diversity and alterna-tives are presented as a normal part of human experience and have a positive value. It promotes what Parekh (1986) calls 'the conscious-ness of alternatives'.

> One cannot then think of anything, be it an activity or form of inquiry, a culture or a society, without at the same time realising that it can be conceptualised or thought about or conducted in several different ways. (p. 123)

The traditional mono-cultural curriculum model tends to promote a cognitive style, which results in choices always being seen as between two alternatives, one of which is right and one of which is wrong. (This is similar to the choice between good and evil.) Virtually all of those involved in anti-racist multiculturalism have been schooled in this tradition. Exposure to different cultural perspectives and an understanding of the nature of racism may have enabled many to throw off the imperial cultural inheritance of Britain's education system without developing 'the consciousness of alternatives' and so retaining a restricted cognitive style.

There has to be a realisation that in a culturally diverse society there are going to be several alternative strategies for promoting that diversity and for combating discriminatory practices and racism through education, employment, unions, health, politics and the law. The exact nature of the particular strategies will vary with time and place. What is appropriate in the early 1990s may be inappropriate in later years, just as what is appropriate in the ethnically mixed context may not be so in the all-white situation. The promotion of anti-racist multiculturalism through the National Curriculum should be seen as just one of several strategies. It does not preclude action by black and Asian parents, or black, Asian and white educationalists in campaigning for fair assessments, for non-ethnocentric resources, for re-presentation on NCC bodies and for the promotion of examples of good practice. Involvement need not mean compliance. It has to be set in a wider context of diverse strategies to ensure that the inequalities which are associated with race, class and gender are continually addressed and are made relevant to all schools. There also has to be a greater awareness of a strategy that has too often been neglected, and that is the issue of pedagogy.

PEDAGOGY

Teaching and learning

Over recent years greater attention has begun to be paid to the teaching and learning styles and their effectiveness in attaining the goals of anti-racist multicultural education.

Grant and Slater (1985) note that the implications of a full acceptance of diversity are considerable and may yet have to be fully appreciated and that 'the teacher directed textbook approach ... is not the appropriate teaching approach for the goals of multicultural education' (p. 111).

Indeed Richards (1986) argues that pedagogy is a priority and not an issue to be tackled only after finding a definition of anti-racism. Richards is not the first to deplore the lack of attention it has received; many classroom teachers would also echo his feeling. There was no guidance in the Swann report and few LEA policy documents mention it. When it has been discussed in the literature it has often been in the context of direct teaching against racism (see Lynch, 1988 and Gaine, 1987). Helpful though this has been, it has also had the effect of marginalising the issues to PSE or Social Science teachers, absolving other staff from involvement or reflection on their own practice.

Both Troyna and Selman (1989) and Carrington and Short (1989a) argue for the wider use of collaborative or co-operative learning techniques. Although much of the work has been conducted in the USA in mixed race settings, the benefits in terms of prejudice reduction, positive feelings about the work and each other seem to be applicable to all schools. In fact, there are claims from evaluations by Slavin (1983) that such learning techniques actually improve academic achievement. Consequently, such techniques can be justified on educational grounds alone, and also as an appropriate vehicle for anti-racist multicultural education.

Troyna and Selman's work (1989) with a variety of FE students, for example, exploring racism within a human rights framework, showed how this could be approached collaboratively and that 'anti-racist education could be implemented successfully in a non-confrontational and constructive manner.'

There is no reason why this kind of approach cannot be extended to classroom explorations of cultural diversity within Britain, especially in the all-white context, examining employment, housing and racism. Within a collaborative learning situation, and with appropriate recources, this should result not just in greater under-standing but also in a commitment to combat racism.

The role of the teacher thus becomes more akin to that of a tutor or facilitator, for as Davey wrote in 1983:

> Purging texts books of black stereotypes, boosting the minority groups in the teaching materials and adjusting the curriculum to accommodate cultural diversity, will have little impact on how children treat each other, if teachers make rules without explanation, if they command needlessly and assume their authority to be established by convention. (p. 182)

There is no doubt that the spread of profiling and records of achievement has often involved a reappraisal of the relationship between teacher and pupil through the management of the learning situation, and a more collaborative style has often been the result. There is a concern, though, that the emphasis on assessment may hinder this approach, with teachers so concerned to reach the attainment targets that they fall back on more didactic methods. However, the NCC appears to emphasise the need for the school to be 'flexible' in delivering the National Curriculum and the time to be devoted to cross-curricular issues would be a further opportunity to explore this. Consequently, collaborative learning situations have to be encouraged on the grounds of good educational practice and as a suitable vehicle to deliver anti-racist multicultural education.

Peer Tutoring

Peer tutoring or cross-age tutoring is sometimes advocated as a method of breaking down barriers between pupils of different ethnic backgrounds and of countering stereotypes. In those schools with few or no pupils from different ethnic backgrounds it may be used as a method for pupils who resist the school's anti-racist ethos because of conflicts this has generated between home and school or between school and some peers. This kind of tutoring may provide a non-threatening, supportive situation in which those pupils can begin to untangle their feelings and come to terms with a very different perspective.

Inter-Ethnic School Exchanges and Contacts

One frequently suggested strategy for all-white schools is for them to develop links with multi-ethnic schools (see Katz and Zalk, 1978). This, it is argued, will lead to greater understanding of cultures and heighten awareness about racism. However, there are dangers in this approach. These kinds of exchanges may confirm stereotypes already held in white pupils' and teachers' minds and most multi-ethnic schools will naturally avoid all-white schools who wish to use them as a 'goldfish bowl'.

Most of the research on and evaluation of these schemes has been conducted in the USA, where certain criteria have been established for successful inter-ethnic contact. These are related to the amount and type of preparation and the nature of the work undertaken during the exchange. Examples of a successful school exchange in a British context are given by Lee, Lee and Pearson (1987) and Grugeon and Woods (1990). The latter describes how the careful preparation by two committed teachers in very different schools led to curriculum developments in English, Maths, Environmental Studies, PE, RE, and PSE, prior to and following a school exchange. Grugeon and Woods (1990) comment:

> New identities were forged as barriers were overcome, confidence established, abilities harnessed, so that several children were seen to do things they have never done before, that some, indeed, suspected they were incapable of doing. This was coupled with the social development involved in the forging of links across regions, across generations and especially across cultures. (p. 139)

They go on to conclude that 'for the promotion of racial harmony, and for learning in general, therefore, such exercises appear to have much to offer' (p. 141). These kinds of schemes are sometimes found in the post-Swann Education Support Grant projects and they should establish relevant criteria within the UK context. Preliminary evaluation of Hampshire's school twinning project (forthcoming 1991) also appears to indicate a positive effect on white pupils' attitudes where it was seen as part of a carefully planned unit of work, where prejudice and racism had been tackled or discussed openly with pupils and staff, and where collaborative activities were jointly planned, giving the opportunity for pupils to work and mix together. In fact some schools' policies have grown out of this experience.

Contact need not always involve exchanges. It can involve letter writing, photography and videoing, all of which can be relevant to attainment targets in core or foundation subjects. Contact can also be international, and two schools in particular, Stantonbury Campus in Milton Keynes and Peers School in Oxford, have documented the effects this has had on the curriculum, pupils and community.

Use can also be made of electronic mailing through Campus 2000, whereby pupils can contact and exchange work with schools abroad.

Exciting though these possibilities are, any sort of contact which involves all-white pupils coming into contact with pupils from another cultural background should take place in what Troyna (1989) refers to as the 'context of a supportive institutional policy' (p. 35). This is the only way to ensure that the experience does not reinforce simplistic stereotypes and that all pupils benefit from the experience.

SUMMARY

There is now a great deal of evidence regarding the inappropriate nature of a mono-cultural curriculum to a culturally diverse society, and that is now recognised by the NCC. However, as pointed out by Carrington and Short (1989b) the appeal of anti-racist multicultural education in all-white schools has to be based on good practice rather than on slogans or rhetoric. Examples of good practice have to be accessible through publicity to Heads, teachers and parents, especially on how such perspectives 'permeate' a topic, because many teachers, in particular, still see this approach as an extra. The work of Troyna and other practitioners, as well as the ESG projects, are part of that process.

The National Curriculum does confer some legitimacy on all-white schools developing multicultural approaches within which anti-racism can operate. The encouragement of cross-curricular initiatives is also in line with anti-racist multicultural developments, especially when using suitable pedagogy. However, the future is not altogether hopeful with possible constraints caused by the use, frequency and possible cultural bias of assessments, opting out and LMS. The damaging effects of these will have to be campaigned against by alert professionals and parents.

There may in some areas be a need for a return to 'warrenism' whereby an individual teacher works hard and slowly for change, although the isolation often experienced by those in that position can be offset by the establishment of local support groups.

Anti-racist multicultural education in multi-ethnic areas will continue to develop due to pressure from black and Asian colleagues and parents, established practice and the community. In all-white areas teachers have to make use of whatever legitimising factors there are, such as the legal, the educational and the moral, in order that the developments of the last few years in these areas are consolidated and built upon.

For many teachers it is the curriculum which offers an obvious way into this approach. Grinter (1990) identifies three main components:

1 The provision of 'knowledge that helps teachers become aware of the ethnocentric nature of the existing curriculum and of the struggles and achievements of Black communities.'

2 Exemplars of effective anti-racist multicultural education related to the National Curriculum.

3 Guidelines for democratic practice in education, involving teachers, students and their communities. However, it is important for teachers to bear in mind that there are, according to Banks (1989), four levels of development related to curricular content.

Level 1 is the Contributions Approach, where other cultures' heroes and holidays are celebrated, but the mainstream curriculum remains unaffected. The issues of racism and sexism are avoided and with the emphasis on the exotica of other cultures this can reinforce existing stereotypes. Its appeal to teachers is that it is easy.

Level 2 is the Cultural Additive approach, which includes additional themes and concepts to the mainstream, curriculum through new books or new units of work.

Level 3 is the Transformation level, where the basic assumptions and pedagogy of the ethnocentric curriculum are being reviewed so that different perspectives are being brought to students from the viewpoint of different ethnic groups or cultures.

Level 4 is the Social Action level. In addition to the above, the curriculum at this level should 'help students to make reflective moral commitments and to take personal, social and civic action that will help create a more just society' (p. 16).

There are now plenty of materials available which relate to Levels 1 and 2. In an attempt to meet the need for materials appropriate to Levels 3 and 4, the Anti-racist Teacher Education Workshops (ARTEW) will be providing a series of exemplars of good practice on Core and Foundation subjects and cross-curricular thematic work which will be of enormous assistance in developing anti-racist multicultural Programmes of Study within the National Curriculum framework.

However, as Banks (1989) points out, you cannot expect teachers at a pre-level 1 stage to jump straight to Level 4. The movement will have to be gradual and cumulative. Consequently, if a more anti-racist multicultural curriculum is to develop effectively through the National Curriculum, this will only be achieved through a carefully managed sequential staff development programme. It is to this rather neglected area that we must now turn.

5

Making and managing change

Although an anti-racist multicultural curriculum is sound educational practice and has been supported for many years by statements from the DES, Government reports and LEA policy statements, there has been little attention paid to the ways in which such a perspective can actually be implemented successfully at LEA and school level. How can policy statements best be translated into good school and classroom practice? What approaches should be avoided? Does the approach depend on the political complexion of the area? What effect does the choice of approach to anti-racism and multiculturalism have in all-white schools? These kinds of questions have usually been avoided in the literature and in LEA policy statements. When they have been acknowledged in the literature it has been in an oblique way with few positive strategies emerging. For instance, Troyna and Williams (1986) recognise this as 'a serious omission' but then devote only one paragraph to a discussion of that 'serious omission'.

Despite the large number of all-white LEAs that now have policy statements, little research has emerged on the effectiveness of these policies in implementing change. A rare example of such research is that conducted by Troyna and Bell (1985) on the development and implementation of 'Milltown's' multicultural education policy.

This policy was also based on the notion of pluralism and stressed the relevance of this for all schools, which have a responsibility to develop a suitable ethos. The changes in the curriculum were to be left to those at the 'chalk face'.

One of the most powerful and influential figures in implementing changes is the Head of the school. In 'Milltown' most did not have any formal training in multicultural education and had been brought up and trained at a time when assimilation or 'colour-blindness' was the dominate paradigm. Although 90 per cent of Heads were in favour of a policy, over one third saw it as irrelevant to them due to their lack of ethnic minority pupils. Schools which claimed to be involved in multicultural education varied considerably in the extent to which they really were involved. It ranged from tokenist religious assemblies to complete curriculum permeation and anti-racism. Such widespread variation in practice reflected the lack of clarity in both academic and policy rhetoric with regard to good multicultural or anti-racist education.

In order to help implement the policy, the authority established a Multicultural Education Unit with three staff. However, its role in the eyes of Heads, teachers and the staff seemed unclear. After three to four years, the Unit had worked in nine of the twelve schools in the sample in Troyna's and Bell's research. The Unit operated on a 'fire brigade' principle. In other words, it responded to calls for help or advice, rather than initiating contact. Consequently, activities were limited to receptive schools. This in turn seemed to confirm the impression, which many Heads and teachers had, that such work was only applicable in those schools which were multiracial. The work of the Unit was also not formally evaluated, which made success and effectiveness impossible to judge.

The authority also appointed an Inspector to develop and co-ordinate multicultural education, not just in schools, but also among the subject and area Inspectors. Troyna and Bell note that this 'was giving practical support and visibility to LEA policy' (p. 23). The LEA also requested that a teacher within the school be given special responsibility for multicultural education. The survey revealed that many of these staff were also unsure of their role.

The research also revealed that, despite the authority's policy, only 5 per cent of the sample schools had declared publicly that multicultural education was part of their aim or philosophy. One reason for this is that, like the Heads, most teachers did not perceive its relevance to all schools. Only 26 per cent saw it as relevant to all institutions and only 2–3 per cent considered it had anything to do with racism. The numerous conclusions from this important piece of research can be summarised as follows:

1 The LEA failed to present multicultural education as good education relevant to all pupils.

2 It failed to define racism and stress the need for all schools to combat manifestation of racism.

3 The policy left implementation to Heads and teachers without giving them sufficient guidance and support on why change was necessary and how it could be organised.

4 The roles of those specifically appointed to develop schools' responses, especially the MEU, were vague, with the consequence that only a handful of receptive schools developed significantly.

5 The lack of co-ordinated INSET ensured that Heads and teachers still perceived the policy to be about the needs of ethnic minorities.

Overall, the experience of this LEA reveals the danger in expecting policies and initiatives themselves to function as change agents. Other LEAs can learn significant lessons from this kind of research and from the experience of LEAs which developed similar policies in the early 1980s.

Schools themselves, such as those quoted in Chapter 1, have responded to a variety of factors, which Gaine (1987) summarises as:

1 Pressure from black and Asian pupils and communities.

2 Right wing political activity in or around the school.

3 A core of committed anti-racist staff, including senior staff.

4 An amalgamation or reorganisation of a school leading to changes in the ethnic composition of the school.

It is unlikely that the majority of all-white schools will be affected by more than one of these factors. Consequently, additional motivation and legitimisation, is needed, such as:

1 Government, NCC and LEA policy statements, which emphasise the role all schools should play in preparing pupils for life in a multicultural society.

2 Examples of good educational practice in a variety of subject areas, which are to be found not just in multiracial schools, but also in all-white schools.

Because the majority of teachers are in all-white schools and their initial training has not addressed the issues of racism, cultural diversity, or the kind of curriculum needed if change to anti-racist multicultural education is to be successful, more attention needs to be paid to staff development. As Lynch (1986) points out:

The generation of a staff development policy for multicultural education is a much more complex and a much more interactive enterprise than that which has been identified by some recent attempts to impose on all teachers attendance at an anti-racist workshop. (p. 150)

Lynch is one of the few writers in the field of multicultural education who tackles the issue of staff development in some detail. For, as he comments, 'however good the policies and policy statements, it is the people who implement them who determine their effectiveness' (p. 145). With so little attention paid to staff development, and bearing in mind that most of the teachers to whom Lynch is referring were trained when the dominant paradigm was assimilation, it is hardly surprising that surveys like those of Troyna and Bell (1985) find a lack of meaningful permeation of multiculturalism.

This issue did receive more attention towards the end of the 1980s with the publication of manuals containing practical ideas for staff training (see Nixon and Watts, 1989, and Maitland, 1989). Gaine (1989) offers a useful series of questions which an institution needs to consider in order to clarify the nature and direction of its policy developments aimed at achieving equal opportunities. The stages of implementation and policy maintenance are also dealt with and bear a close resemblance to the process outlined in Chapter 6. In a valuable contribution to the understanding of managing whole school change, Pauline Lyseight-Jones (1989) details the lessons learned from many INSET courses organised in the mid to late 1980s. Her perspective shows an awareness of the reality of staffroom life and there are useful sections on dealing with opposition, finding allies, feelings of isolation, disseminating information and planning INSET. Perhaps the most important conclusion offered by Lyseight-Jones is that: 'Incorrect or inadequate definition of the issue will lead to inappropriate outcomes. At best such an outcome could be called tokenism' (p. 39).

It is finding the appropriate method of arriving at such a definition with teachers and a school, as well as the most effective strategies for further development, which has so often been neglected in the literature and policy documents.

In an attempt to tackle this, Lynch (1986a) has suggested a 'typology of staff development' which covers six areas which would have to be addressed for effective multicultural and anti-racist developments.

1 *The cultural and contextual:* this includes the development of a heterogeneous staff and inter-ethnic contacts.

2 *The moral/affective:* the development of a public commitment to and ethos of anti-racist multicultural education.

3 *The cognitive:* combating the ignorance on which a lot of prejudice is built.

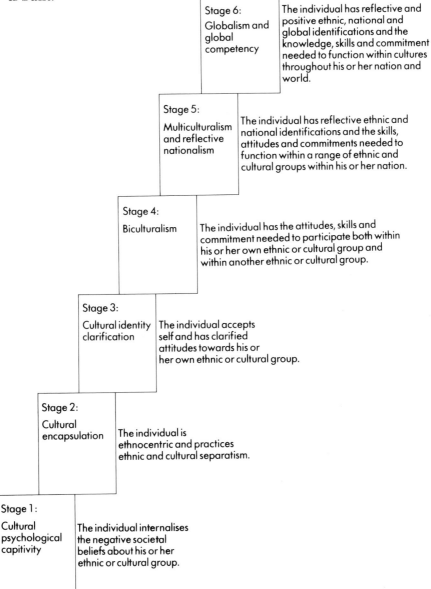

Stage 6:
Globalism and global competency

The individual has reflective and positive ethnic, national and global identifications and the knowledge, skills and commitment needed to function within cultures throughout his or her nation and world.

Stage 5:
Multiculturalism and reflective nationalism

The individual has reflective ethnic and national identifications and the skills, attitudes and commitments needed to function within a range of ethnic and cultural groups within his or her nation.

Stage 4:
Biculturalism

The individual has the attitudes, skills and commitment needed to participate both within his or her own ethnic or cultural group and within another ethnic or cultural group.

Stage 3:
Cultural identity clarification

The individual accepts self and has clarified attitudes towards his or her own ethnic or cultural group.

Stage 2:
Cultural encapsulation

The individual is ethnocentric and practices ethnic and cultural separatism.

Stage 1:
Cultural psychological capitivity

The individual internalises the negative societal beliefs about his or her ethnic or cultural group.

Figure 2 *The stages of ethnic and cultural development*

4 *The pedagogical performance:* the specific teaching and in-structional behaviours and professional attitudes necessary for multicultural developments.

5 *The consequential:* the behaviour and attitudes of staff and pupils that would be expected as a result of commitment to anti-racist multicultural education.

6 *The experiential:* the experiences and insights gained by staff through working with or in ethnic minority communities.

In deciding how these should be addressed, Banks (1981) points out that all teachers, whatever their race, ethnic group or social class background, will not benefit to the same extent from identical training strategies. It is necessary to take account of cultural experiences, personality and levels of knowledge in deciding how to address staff development. As an aid to this, Banks has developed a typology which attempts to outline the stages of cultural or ethnic development which are revealed by teachers and students (see Figure 2 – *Source: Multi-ethnic Education: Theory and Practice*).

Banks is suggesting that teachers are not really ready for powerful, affective techniques such as Racial Awareness Training (RAT) until they have reached Stage 3. Initial staff development should therefore aim at moving teachers from Stage 1 to Stage 3. This is particularly applicable to all-white schools, where contact with ethnic minority pupils and other cultures is low. Banks makes a central point:

> I am suggesting that until teachers come to grips with their own personal and cultural identities and are comfortable with them, it will be difficult for them to develop empathy with the experiences of victimised racial and cultural groups. (p. 17)

RACISM AWARENESS TRAINING

RAT grew out of Human Awareness Training, which developed during the 1960s. The race riots which took place in the late 1960s in several American cities were mirrored by racial incidents in eleven Army bases and major incidents at Marine bases in Japan. The deep-seated racial animosity this revealed was potentially very damaging to the cohesion and effectiveness of the military. The US military began developing courses in race relations which, according to Peppard (1983), developed into a 16-week awareness training course, covering personal and institutional racism.

Meanwhile the Kerner Commission (1968) into the riots emphasised the role of white people in creating and perpetuating racism, stressing that combating racism involved 'changing the behaviour of whites' and that this was the principle responsibility of the white community.

Following the Commission's report and the experiments in the US military, there developed a host of literature and programmes in education, psychology and the churches, dealing with the white psyche and white behaviour. The aim was to create a 'new white consciousness through attitudinal and behavioural change'. This type of work culminated in J. Katz's *White Awareness: A Handbook for Anti-racism Training* (1978). Katz's work and approach has considerably influenced RAT programmes in Britain.

The book grew, according to Katz, out of her own personal and professional struggle to understand and come to grips with racism. It is meant as an attempt to help white people break out of the role of aggressor, as they are also seen as 'suffering' from racism. This is perhaps expressed most effectively by Du Bois (1920):

> Am I, in my blackness, the sole sufferer? I suffer – and yet, somehow above the suffering, above the shackled anger that breaks the bars, above the hurt that crazes, there surges in me a vast pity – pity for a people imprisoned and enthralled, hampered and made miserable for such a cause, for such a phantasy.

The effect of racism on whites in the US Commission on Mental Health (1965) is referred to as a 'most compelling health hazard' as it 'cripples the growth and development of millions of our citizens'.

Since the 1960s, racism has been seen by some as a form of schizophrenia, in that there is a large gap between what whites believe in and what they actually practise. This causes them to live in a state of psychological stress. As long ago as 1944 Myrdal, in *The American Dilemma*, was pointing out the schisms between:

> American ideals of equality, freedom, the God given dignity of individuals' inalienable rights on the one hand against practices of discrimination, humiliation, insult, denial or opportunity in a racist society on the other. (Quoted in Katz, 1978, p. 12)

Psychiatrists such as Comer (1972) see racism as a disease deeply rooted in personality, from which Katz concludes that 'racism is a critical and pervasive form of mental illness'. One of the manifestations of this is the 'white is right' attitude combined with a reluctance to see oneself as white. A white person when asked about his or her 'race' will usually reply 'English', 'Italian' or 'Jewish'; rarely will the answer be 'white'. Katz argues that seeing oneself as an individual unwilling to 'own' one's whiteness is a way of denying responsibility for perpetuating a racist system.

The disease of racism also cripples people intellectually, in the sense that white children are miseducated through the constant reinforcement of white, Anglow-Saxon history, invention, enterprise and culture. As Johnson (1950) puts it:

> Can you name a single one of the great fundamental and intellectual achievements which have raised man in the scale of civilization that may be credited to the Anglo-Saxon? The art of letters, of poetry, of music, of sculpture, of painting, of drama, of architecture; the sciences of mathematics, of astronomy, of philosophy, of logic, of physics, of chemistry; the use of metals and the principles of mechanics, were all invented or discovered by darker and what we now call inferior races and nations ... Do you know that the only original contribution to civilization we can claim is in what we have done in steam and electricity and in making implements of war more deadly?

According to Katz and others, the roots of racist thinking and their development among whites go back, at least within the American context, 350 year to the time when the first Europeans landed in the New World, with a host of negative associations towards black people, together with the assumed natural superiority of white civilisation. The subsequent treatment of the American Indian, the introduction of civil war over slavery, and the doctrine of manifest destiny all bear witness to the assumed superiority of the white race. Such a long history of oppression of other races has resulted in racism being deeply embedded in the white psyche. It is part of the psycho-social history of whites, part of its collective unconscious embodied in white American customs, institutions and language. It is both overt and covert, often at the same time. There is no escaping it.

Such a pervasive ideology will obviously be very resistant to change and Katz's concern is precisely the lack of change, despite the civil rights campaigns. Multicultural policies have not penetrated white areas where 'cultural isolation may be greatest' (p. 8) and until 'the real perpetuators of racism are confronted, and educated, little will change'.

The training programme devised by Katz attempts to bring individual whites to a consciousness of themselves, their culture and institutions operating at two levels: the cognitive or informative and the affective or emotional. The programme takes the form of an intense, well-structured day or two-day session, experientially based with self-reflexive group work. The aim is to gain insights into personal and institutional racism, encouraging further affirmative action.

The appeal of such programmes in Britain was that they did actually tackle the issue of racism. The demand for such courses intensified after the riots in British cities in 1981, especially in inner city areas for a variety of personnel: policy makers, housing officers, teachers and health workers. Since the publication of the Swann Report and its emphasis on education for all, there may be a demand for such courses among inspectors, Heads and teachers in all-white areas. Indeed, RAT is frequently recommended as a way of arousing and moving individuals quickly to a recognition of personal and institutional racism. Swann and others have noted the frequent remark amongst staff in all-white schools that 'there is no problem here'. Racism's existence is acknowledged, but always somewhere else. Given this background, RAT is seen as 'one quick and effective way to raise the consciousness of such people'.

The needs of all-white schools and strategies for them have been outlined by Twitchin (1985). What is required is a move to an anti-racist overt curriculum and a non-racist hidden curriculum. This process can take up to five years and involve the whole staff, including an intensive well-structured RAT course. As Gaine (1987) remarks 'it is not sufficient to simply give the correct information or correct certain myths when attempting to change attitudes and behaviour'. In all-white schools the issue of racism may be new, and may provoke defensive reactions among teachers if the trainer is following Katz's confrontational approach. As Gaine notes, 'people do not learn or change attitudes or change actions when they feel attacked, defensive, hostile, angry or guilty'. For this reason, a 'softly, softly' approach is usually recommended, and Twitchin suggests the use of an outside adviser for the initial stage of racism awareness, where whites can reflect on the nature of racial injustice. The aim is, according to Twitchin, not to confront people but the issue. There is obviously a very fine line and one made doubly precarious by the assumption underlying Katz's approach, that an observer, one who has stood idly by, is a racist – that being white itself implies being racist.

Twitchin stresses the need for the group leader in RAT sessions to create a non-threatening atmosphere. For those following Katz's principles, this is very difficult. The emphasis is on the need for white people to help dismantle structural barriers to equality, ensuring that their actions support the active resistance of the black oppressed and do not serve to 'contain' that resistance. RAT should be seen as a step in this direction, as it addresses the needs of all children in a 'multicultural, multiracial society, characterised by racial disadvantage and widespread discrimination'. It should also spur people on to action in combating personal and institutional racism.

The kind of action usually envisaged within the context of a school is the setting up of a working party with representatives from all areas of the curriculum. This seeks the active support of the whole staff, governors and representatives of the community, as it works its way towards a whole-school policy on a multicultural curriculum and procedures and strategies to combat racism attitudes, behaviour and practices within the school. This has been the policy of those schools in multiracial areas which have tackled the issue and published statements of policies on this matter – a practice endorsed by the Swann Report. RAT's appeal is therefore considerable in developing this process.

The appeal of RAT is often characterised as a solution to the liberal establishment's moral opposition to racism. But it goes further than that because it also appeals to black and Asian people, as it seems to force whites to recognise black oppression and to offer programmes to overcome it. Sivanandan (1985) argues that it also appeals to the State, particularly in the field of law and order, where a better informed and trained police force should be able to carry out its functions more effectively.

With such a wide-ranging appeal, it is surprising that the theoretical under-pinnings have only recently been examined. According to Gurmah (1984), they consist of a mixture of Marxist sociology and Rogerian psychology. Thus the definition of racism employed by Katz encompasses the socio-economic development of industrial capitalism, together with the Rogerian notion of an actual and ideal self concept. Rogerian theory stress the innate goodness of the self, its desire for knowledge and growth and its wish to be whole and integrated. However, for a variety of reasons, ignorance or anxiety, the self may reject part of itself, although these disassociated parts are still incorporated in the self. Part of Rogerian 'client-centred' therapy is to encourage the patient to discover for himself or herself the disassociated parts, in order to achieve a complete integration of the self. The cure for racism is seen as resolving the discrepancy between an individual's actual and ideal self concepts, i.e. the schism that exists between holding and practising racist ideas within a supposedly tolerant, democratic and Christian society. This is what has led Katz and others to see racism as a form of mental illness deeply embedded in the white psyche. However, as Gurmah (1984) asks, why should people be defined as mentally disturbed simply because they are racist, or sexist? What they are really doing is affronting the concept of an ideal person.

According to Katz, racism manifests itself in pain, guilt and fear. As with most mental illnesses, it is emotionally and intellectually immobilising. Yet, if this is so, how is it that white people have so much political, economic and social power while suffering so much? Gurmah argues that such white people are, in fact, equipped better in psychological and material terms, as they are in a position to define and control the kind of reality experienced by black people. Gurmah concludes that RAT is theoretically inadequate, making too many unsubstantiated jumps, metaphysical and reductionist. What RAT misses is that racism is a relationship and that 'one cannot fruitfully focus on the nature of the individual in the hope of solving structural inequalities'.

Sivanandan (1985) also suggests that this neglect of the relationship of racism to the social hierarchy is a flight from the connection between race and class. Racism is not a white problem, but a problem of 'an exploitative white power structure; power is not something white people are born into, but that which they derive from their position in a complex sex/class hierarchy' (p. 27). RAT consequently reduced social problems to individual solutions and confuses personal satisfaction with political liberation. For instance, those who have undergone RAT in housing departments cannot change the housing conditions of the black working class as long as the housing stock and finance is limited or controlled elsewhere.

Katz's notion of the historic roots of racism which has now become part of the collective unconscious means that white people can never become anything other than anti-racist racists. Sivanandan points out that this a circular argument, bordering on the genetic, and criticises RAT for its ragbag notions of 'mental illness, original sin and biological determinism' (p. 29). For what RAT ignores: is the important factor of the material conditions which breed racism. This, according to Sivanandan in particular, is why RAT has directed itself towards professional middle-class groups or avoided the white working class, which is racist precisely because it is powerless economically and politically and violent because the only power it has is personal power. It would therefore be very difficult to change the attitudes and behaviour of the white working class without first changing the material conditions of its existence. But here, as Sivanandan (1985) puts it, 'RAT averts its face' (p. 30).

For those professional groups who do not enter RAT sessions, the experience may be more akin to a mild religious revivalist meeting or a self-help group, where individuals 'confess' their 'sin' of racism to everyone, but most of all to themselves. Despite attempts to establish a non-threatening atmosphere, the tone, as Gurmah (1984) notes, is frequently accusatory and highly moralistic. The idea is to 'guilt trip' white people into action, yet, at the same time, to taunt them with the notion that they can only ever become anti-racist racists. They can only ever assist blacks in their struggle, never play a major part in the action.

Although Katz and others make frequent reference to the white psyche, no mention is made of the black psyche. For instance, what scars and attitudes have centuries of slavery, forced removals, colonialism, humiliation, abuse, poverty and discrimination left in the black collective consciousness, apart from the obvious desire to escape such an oppressive situation? What consequences does this have on the ability of black and Asian people to escape from the role of the oppressed, and to what extent can the ideas of equality and justice be realised? One interesting question not tackled is whether, under Katz's definitions, blacks can be racist if they gain positions of power and influence. Such questions are avoided by RAT's insistence on racism being solely a white problem.

Despite these criticisms, RAT has been in increasing demand, but the spur for this case came not so much from the established effectiveness of such sessions, but rather from a desire by many professional groups to be seen to be doing something positive following the riots in inner cities during 1981.

Consequently, these developments have not been universally welcomed, especially by black and Asian people. Gurmah (1984) is concerned that RAT gives white officials the acceptable language of anti-racism with which to disarm black criticisms. Sivanandan (1985) argues that RAT's reduction of social problems to individual solutions is a useful way for the State to smooth out social discontent while it carries on untramelled with its capitalistic works (p. 20).

In addition to this notion of State management of crises, there is the doubt expressed about the ethics of commercialisation, which is now a feature of RAT, especially through fairly expensive programmes. The fear is that commercialisation implies the compromising of the message or content, depending on who is paying the fee, and a tendency for organisations to see RAT as a panacea for professional bodies, leading to token gestures.

Gurmah and Sivanandan both conclude that RAT tends to be misused, as it appeals to people's guilt; is wasted effort, as it is ineffective; and is harmful as it can be appropriated by the State, as well as separating the issue of race from that of class. Sivanandan sees it as 'degrading the black struggle'.

Despite these criticisms, both writers recognise the commitment and optimism of many trainers and ackowledge that RAT may act as a catalyst for certain guilt-stricken whites. However, it may be that such people had the potential to change anyway, and the assumption that RAT can do more is 'a delusion of grandeur' (Sivanandan, 1985 p. 28). It cannot do more because there is no 'clear strategic route from this kind of consciousness raising session to political action' (Gurmah, 1984, p. 18).

The Swann report, in considering the relevance of RAT to all-white schools, whilst in agreement with the objectives of RAT, expressed doubts about its value. It was felt that many undergoing such training were already likely to be committed to anti-racism and that there was need for more research into these programmes, especially on evaluation. The report concluded that RAT:

> May have less chance of effectively influencing the attitudes and behaviour of a teacher who has not previously considered this aspect of his/her work than would a longer, more broadly based in-service course which sets racism in a wider perspective. (p. 588)

But it is just this kind of in-service training which is lacking in all-white areas. Although a few LEAs may take some steps to improve the situation (for example, through policy statements), it is likely that the needs of the National Curriculum, and concerns over assessments, profiling and LMS will take precedence in most schools. It may therefore rest with individual schools and concerned teachers to attempt to put some of the recommendations of *Education for All* and LEA's policies into practice.

The suggestions of the critics of RAT amount to Gurmah's advice that 'in all schools and colleges, teachers can examine the content of their curriculum and interfere with those colleagues who teach racist material'.

There is more to challenging established patterns and practices in schools which have not considered the issue of racism than boldly stating that they should do and interfering with colleagues whose material is perceived as racist. The defensive, perhaps even hostile, reaction which RAT can provoke (criticised by Gurmah and others) is even more likely if Gurmah's rather blunt approach is adopted.

Galliers (1987) argues that many of Sivanandan's and Gurmah's criticisms are based on a misrepresentation of RAT and do not stand up, and that there is no reason for abandoning RAT. Galliers points out that Katz does stress that the workshops are a beginning, not a finished product, and that it is not claimed that they change attitudes. This misrepresentation of RAT continued with the way in which some of Gaine's comments on RAT have been used to devalue its use, especially in the all-white situation. Gaine (1987) did actually point out that there are a wide range of techniques that go under the RAT label. Some focus on the personal, others on the political and institutional. Gaine argued against those techniques which only put people through a mild trauma, making them feel guilty but somehow better about the situation. In fact, Gaine argued that RAT did have a part to play in a sequential development plan which addressed all aspects of racism in education, and that RAT certainly did not rule out democratic action.

Very few accounts have been written by RAT practitioners (Gaine is one), and those that exist reveal a degree of thought which is unexpected in the light of some of the savage criticisms.

As organisers of RAT workshops, Gledhill and Hefferman (1984) state that they were mindful of the pitfalls of unadulterated 'soul bearing and counter productive guilt raising' and that 'we have tended to place a greater emphasis on the institutional dimension' (p. 47). They, like other providers, attempt to work at several levels:

the personal, the cultural, the historical and the institutional. Their approach is also linked to what is happening in participants' own professional settings and aims to produce a plan of action.

The misrepresentation to which Galliers refers seems to have focused heavily on one particular part of RAT, the personal, and on one or two methodologies which even practitioners themselves question.

Burtonwood (1986) defends the inclusion of the personal on such courses by arguing that it is essential to confront ourselves, to examine and reflect upon how we habitually operate and manage situations, if change is to occur. In his review of multicultural and anti-racist INSET, Burtonwood noticed how racist generalisations were common among course participants and that many were firmly committed to an assimilation framework. This is a finding confirmed by Carrington and Short (1989b). If racist views and their origins are not to be examined, there is little chance of any meaningful personal and professional growth. However, Grant and Grant (1985) note how difficult it is to eliminate ethnic stereotyping among course participants, and no amount of haranguing or finger pointing is likely to achieve this. Carrington and Short argue that a full-scale assault on such an individual will be rejected, because the new position offered will currently be outside his or her 'latitude of acceptance'. Consequently, there may be no alternative than to examine and make use of the kind of RAT which has been effective in dealing with personal racial constructs, by taking people through a series of gentle stages from one position to another.

Galliers (1987) suggests that the 'here and now' focus of Katz's techniques needs to merge with a 'there and then' element which connects to the wider social and economic structure. The skillful use of T-groups will, according to research in the USA, produce positive attitudinal and behavioural changes.

When people feel secure in small groups, RAT techniques can move them, argues Gaine. This applies especially to the all-white situation, where people will not be radicalised or have their awareness raised by race issues inside the classroom. The effectiveness of such an approach is described in Abbott et al (1989) where a small group of Heads undertook a three day anti-racist workshop which did result in a positive reassessment of their perspectives and a commitment to action. In echoing Myrdal (1944), Gaine (1987) argues that RAT can work with professional educators because 'it highlights a tension between many professed beliefs, personal and institutional, and actual practice' (p. 114).

After all, how do you raise the awareness and gain the commitment of those colleagues who:

1 In their childhood and professional adult life have not been in the same room as a black or Asian person.

2 Despite having had some contact with members of ethnic minorities have never really 'listened' to them.

3 Were raised in the 1950s and 1960s in areas with an increasing ethnic minority population, which seemed to cause 'problems' and where prejudice and racism went unchallenged.

4 Have only experience black people in a colonial context.

5 Have had no initial or subsequent training in these matters.

6 Whose image of ethnic minorities and anti-racist multicultural education has to some extent been formed by the media.

These are just a few of the experiences which individuals bring to INSET and they are not always confined to the all-white situation, although they are more often found in those circumstances. What is essential is that such experiences are recognised and dealt with not in an accusatory way but rather in a secure non-judgemental context, which then provides a firmer base for personal and professional growth.

However, the danger of confirming a stereotype of the white teacher must be avoided. Over recent years there has been a slow but steady trickle of teachers, Heads and Inspectors out of those LEAs who pioneered much of the early work in this field, and they bring a depth of knowledge and expertise which has contributed to the growth of some good practice in all-white situations.

Another criticism of RAT and similar courses has been the underlying assumption that persuading people of the desirability of something, in this case anti-racist multicultural education for all, is sufficient to make it happen.

In order for change at an institutional level to take place, as Galliers (1987) points out, the status of the learner is very important and, if he or she is alone, then change can be difficult to promote at whole-school level. Indeed, Grant and Grant (1985) state quite simply that the support of the Head is essential for change to take place. This has led to many courses recruiting two senior staff from each of a small number of schools with a prior understanding with the Heads of these schools that changes will be expected.

Getting both the numbers and the status of participants right, recognising what they may be bringing to the situation, and devising appropriate unlearning and relearning techniques will not bring about whole-school changes. In his review (1986), Burtonwood noted that courses 'rarely included a consideration of the change process itself'. Any INSET has to provide participants with an understanding of the change process in schools and equip them with skills and strategies to effect change, so that whole-school developments can take place and anti-racist multiculturalism can permeate all aspects of institutional life.

But what kind of strategies can be employed, in which a form of RAT may play a part? If we are aiming at change occurring at a personal, professional and institutional level, then we have to be more aware of the mechanisms and processes involved in promoting change in individual schools.

Chin and Benne (1976) have identified three types or groups of strategies which can be used in promoting change. The first of these, the empirical-rational, rests on the underlying assumption that all men and women are rational and so when change is necessary it can be achieved and justified by an appeal to rationality and the benefits it will bring to the recipients. The second of these, normative-re-educative, recognises the above but stresses that change has to be more than cognitive. It usually involves a change of normative orientations, involving a re-appraisal of attitudes, values, skills and significant relationships. The third strategy relied on power-coercive methods whereby change is affected through laws or administrative policy, i.e. a very top-down approach. Such strategies can be used 'without much awareness on the part of those out of power in the system that such strategies are being employed' (p. 40). However, Chin and Benne also point out that this approach may result in opposition which takes the form of refusal to cooperate and/or strikes.

Whatever strategies are employed and emphasised will depend on the particular issue involved and the context. How this relates to the development of anti-racist multicultural education will be referred to a little later.

David (1982) details four caveats to be born in mind when change in institutions is being proposed.

> One assumption is that change does not occur unless the particulars of a school and its context are taken into account.
>
> A second is that school staff will not be committed to a change effort unless they have had the opportunity to be involved in decisions concerning the shape of this project.
>
> A third is that effective schools are characterised by a school-wide focus – a set of shared goals and a unified approach to instruction as opposed to several separate coordinated projects and approaches.
>
> Finally, proponents of school-based strategies believe that any planning effort that encourages self-awareness and reflection on the part of school staff will greatly increase the chances that behaviours will change.

Indeed, Hopkins (1986), in reviewing studies on teacher in-service training, suggests that school-based activities are more suited where complex teacher behaviours are involved. Of course the implementation of an anti-racist multicultural curriculum is just such a task and involves teachers recognising the limitations and dangers of a monocultural curriculum. We also, however, need to remember one of Guskey's (1986) guiding principles, which is that change is a gradual and difficult process for teachers.

If the process is to begin and develop, then Lynch suggests that staff development should focus on the three areas of:

1 The cognitive

2 The affective

3 The behavioural (conative).

Lynch suggests that a staff-development programme should address these domains by the inclusion of the following factors.

Cognitive

Participants need to be aware of the extent of local and national diversity, theories of prejudice acquisition and reduction, appropriate pedagogies, legislation, familiarity with other cultures.

Affective

Participants need to develop respect for persons, commitment to combating prejudice and discrimination, personal and professional evaluation, high expectation of all pupils.

Behavioural (conative)

Participants need to develop skills in encouraging non-prejudiced attitudes and behaviour, dismantling prejudiced attitudes, expertise in inter-cultural contacts, a critical reflective approach, recognising and combating racism in and out of school.

Before considering the content of a staff-development programme which attempts to meet these aims, and is the subject of the following chapter, it is worth bearing in mind some of the findings of research into teacher in-service training. Those that seem pertinent to anti-racist multicultural education are the following:

1 One-shot workshops are ineffective.

2 There is a need for support and follow-up.

3 Teachers learn best from other teachers.

4 Teachers' everyday experiences, should be utilised.

5 Demonstrations should be made of the positive effects to be had on the curriculum and on pupils' learning.

6 An emphasis should be placed on good practice – teachers should not be attacked for bad practice.

7 The need for an overall plan of change should be stressed.

8 The existence of overall policy objectives nationally and at LEA level can be effective.

From what we can learn from the theory and practice of educational change, there are certain principles which should underly any staff-development programme related to anti-racist multicultural education:

1 There is a need for normative re-educative change to take place within a framework of empirical-rational and power-coercive measures.

2 There needs to be a combined approach which observes cognitive, affective and conative domains and which extends teachers' professional skills relevant to education in a multicultural society (e.g. recognising bias, racism, ethnocentrism and how to combat these). RAT may form a part of this.

3 The goal should be of a whole-school commitment to the enriching qualities of cultural pluralism, combating racism individually and institutionally.

4 An assessment should be made of the power structure of the institution and where the school and its staff have reached in terms of their knowledge, experience and attitudes towards anti-racist multicultural education.

5 There should be the creation of a 'sense of ownership' of the change of policies, through open democratic dialogue and the involvement of teachers in each stage of development. (Although the involvement may initially be restricted to teachers, it also has to include non-teaching staff, pupils, parents and the wider community.)

6 Participants need to be aware that it is not going to be quick or easy to bring about change.

The six principles above can be translated into a staff-development programme which could take the form of the model in Figure 3, but will of course vary from school to school depending on the institution's starting point.

WORKING PARTIES

Duncan (1986), as Head of Wyck Manor, related how the working party's role was seen as starting off and then co-ordinating developments. An outsider was used to introduce the issue into the school and this was followed by a series of micro or specialist lectures to faculties and subject heads.

Duncan's account and other accounts, such as Peter Mitchell's (1984) tend to imply that it is a very straightforward path from raising the issue, developing awareness and forming a policy, to implementing change. Most examples of this process are in multiracial schools, where the staff see the relevance of attempts to improve ethnic minority achievement or combat racism. The situation in all-white schools is obviously rather different, lacking those immediate concerns, and therefore there is a need for a considered programme of staff development before considering the extent of change.

For any working party on multicultural education to have a chance of being successful, it is essential that:

Time-scale | Stage | Development

1   *Legitimacy and awareness of demand for action* – from Swann, LEA policy, GCSE criteria, National Curriculum, parents/governors; racial incidents in or around school.

2   *Gaining commitment for need for action* – from Head, senior staff; open dialogue, staff meetings, curriculum meetings, etc.; finding support.

3   *Planning a coherent strategy* – establishing goals and working group/party with open invitation.

1½ years

4   *Awareness-raising of change agents* – understanding of issues, concepts; familiarity with literature; contacting and visiting other teachers and schools; encouragement for INSET for working group/party.

5   *Researching, gathering evidence, assessing the school* – staff survey of knowledge, training; what is already being done; survey of languages or cultural backgrounds of school and area; evidence of racist attitudes or incidents amongst pupils; looking at curriculum materials; reports to staff.

6   *Staff development* – (a) awareness-raising strategies; analysing, identifying the problem; how can it be solved? What part can we play as teachers and a school?
(b) Acquiring skills and competence for anti-racist multi-cultural education.
(c) Evaluation and feedback of feelings and developments.

1½ to 3 years

7   *Policy formulation* – whole-school involvement, as effects whole institution; ethos and curriculum.

8   *Policy negotiation* – with whole staff, governors and pupils.

9   *Dissemination* – pupils, parents and the community.

3 to 5 years

10   *Implementation* – with constant monitoring and reviewing.

Figure 3 *Model 5-year staff-development programme*

1 The working party is seen as legitimate, being proposed or supported by the Head.

2 It involves senior management, various other representatives of the management structure and a full range of subject-area representatives.

3 It has to find ways of discussing sensitive issues. However, as Nixon (1985) points out, 'differences of opinion don't always have to be resolved.'

4 It clarifies as far as possible the immediate aims and the issues involved. This should include some personal involvement in a form of RAT and greater familiarity with the literature.

5 The working party gains support from other schools and advisers.

6 It keeps the rest of the staff informed about its aims, directions and progress through regular bulletins and reports at staff meetings.

7 It monitors staff views on the issues through discussion and formal questionnaires. It must be borne in mind that many teachers will feel threatened and defensive about matters relating to racism and prejudice, and they will sometimes interpret the raising of these as a form of personal and professional criticism. This can result in a consolidation of resistance to change.

8 A programme of staff development is created based on an accurate assessment of the needs of the staff and the traditions of innovation in the particular school.

As Lyseight-Jones (1989) points out:

> The working party's first task is to educate itself . . . The working party's self-education process may show the aware that they have further to go and the complacent that they have touched only the tip of the iceberg . . . [and that they] will have learned things which other colleagues have yet to grasp or encounter. Excessive zeal will alienate as will being a benevolent oppressor. (p. 43)

SUMMARY

In the immediate aftermath of the Swann Report there was a considerable amount of LEA activity in developing and promoting anti-racist or multicultural policies. This sometimes took the form of racism-awareness workshops for Heads and teachers. A few LEAs introduced deadlines for school policies and guidelines on what these should cover. However, most of the time an important element was missing, just as it had been in the Swann Report, and that was advice on how the change or developments were to be managed by staff, pupils and the community.

This was tragically highlighted in September 1986 by the murder of 13-year-old Ahmed Iqbal Ullah by a white pupil in the playground of Burnage High School, Manchester and the subsequent polarisation which took place in the community along racial lines. An inquiry was set up by Manchester City Council and led by Ian Macdonald QC, but the final report ran into publication problems when the council refused to publish the report in full. It was concerned that parts of the report were defamatory and exposed the council to libel action. Some of the report was leaked to the press, parts of which interpreted the information as proof that the school's anti-racist policy had contributed to the death of Ahmed and the polarisation of the community. However, this was far from the case and a statement made later by Ian Macdonald on behalf of the inquiry team made this clear:

> We repudiate totally any suggestion that the anti-racist education policy in Burnage High School led either to the death of Ahmed Ullah or to the disturbances in March 1987. Far from suggesting that Burnage High School and other schools should abandon strategies for combating racism and adopt a 'colour-blind' approach, we state emphatically that the work of all schools should be informed by a policy that recognised the pernicious and all-pervasive nature of racism in the lives of students, teachers and parents, black and white, and the need to confront it. We further emphasise that this is not only a task facing schools in inner cities or in what some people still insist on calling 'immigrant areas'. It is incumbent upon schools and colleges everywhere to tackle the issue of racism in the same way as they recognise the need to accept the technological revolution and prepare students to be technically competent in an age of new technology.

The report was finally published at the team's own expense in January 1990. It emphasised the need for participation of the whole school community in the creation and implementation of anti-racist policies.

It was critical of what it termed 'moral' or 'symbolic' anti-racism. In this model the problem is still seen as meeting the special needs of ethnic minority pupils. This was done at Burnage through a separate Community Education Department, dependent on Section 11 funding. Parents' advisory groups were set up for Afro-Caribbean and Asian parents but not for white. Much of the basis for the policies at Burnage seemed to rest on the dubious notions of endemic white racism as purveyed in some of the RAT courses criticised earlier. The result of this was ethnic segregation. White and Afro-Caribbean pupils were even prevented from attending Ahmed Iqbal Ullah's funeral. The report goes on to suggest that the school's notion of 'community' appeared to exclude the white working class and encouraged the feeling that black and Asian pupils were receiving special treatment and hence fueling a white backlash.

A significant criticism was the way in which these developments had been managed over the years which can be categorised as a 'top down' approach. The report called for greater involvement of all parents, staff, ancillaries and governors of all ethnic origins as well as students themselves in the development of any policies related to anti-racist multicultural issues.

The following chapter deals with one school's attempts to put some of the theories of the successful management of change outlined here into practice, not as a definitive guide (it predates the Macdonald report) but as one contribution to a developing set of strategies, especially relevant to the all-white situation.

6

Theory into practice: the Frogmore experience

One example of an attempt to put some of these theories and ideas into practice is the experience of Frogmore Community School. The school is 99 per cent white and situated in what is referred to in the school booklet as a 'semi-rural part of North-East Hampshire'.

For several years a small group of teachers had become concerned about the negative and hostile racial attitudes held by many of the white pupils. These attitudes seemed to go unchallenged throughout the years of schooling and, when they were challenged, seemed to remain impervious to change. This led to some individual teachers questioning their own responses to overt manifestations of racism in class and to a consideration of how their curriculum might contribute to these negative and hostile attitudes.

What was important was that these concerns were also shared by the Head of the school, who agreed to the setting up of a working party in early 1985 which would examine all the issues and report regularly to the Head and staff.

As Nixon (1985) points out, the composition of any working party is very important if it is to gain credibility in the eyes of staff. It must therefore involve senior management and, to avoid marginalisation, has to establish formal means of communicating its ideas to the rest of the staff.

As membership of the working party was to be voluntary, it was fortunate that those who were interested included both Deputy Heads, a Youth and Community Worker who worked on the site, a Head of House with teaching responsibility in Science, a teacher of Mathematics, the Head of the Humanities Faculty and the Heads of Modern Languages, Drama and Personal and Social Education. Thus the only areas of the curriculum unrepresented were CDT and PE.

The early meetings of the working party were taken up by agreements over aims and priorities, while also familiarising the participants more thoroughly with the issues involved in multi-culturalism and anti-racism. This involved not only discussing matters amongst ourselves but also attending courses (such as the one described by Marina Foster, 1986), conferences, writing to and meeting advisers, lecturers and representatives of various organisations. We were also able to arrange visits for some members of the working party to multi-ethnic schools which had developed whole-school policies and major curriculum initiatives.

From this flurry of activity emerged a recognition that:

1 If any meaningful change was to occur it had to involve the whole school in an examination of attitudes, curriculum content and institutional practices.

2 The approach developed in multicultural schools may not be appropriate to all-white schools.

At that time there did not appear to be any schools in the white highlands who had developed policies, nor were there all-white schools within multi-ethnic LEAs who had policy statements. Undoubtedly there are a number of reasons for this, including a degree of institutional racism, but the policies themselves were set in the context of the needs and entitlement of ethnic minorities in multi-ethnic settings. How this was also relevent to the curriculum and ethos of the mainly white schools was often ignored. Consequently there were few experiences on which we could directly draw. This forced us into considering and analysing our own school in great detail, staff and pupils, before undertaking any in-service work. For example, we were conscious that although some pupils would express openly racist views, there were many more who, as Cochrane and Billig (1984) identified, did not 'hold the unambiguous views of the crude bigot'. These pupils would profess a belief in the importance of tolerance and admit that prejudice was wrong. Racist views were presented with a certain respectability and the necessity of the expulsion of non-whites was expressed with regret. However such actions were seen as inevitable due to the immigrants' unwillingness to give up their customs and religion and to prevent further unemployment.

We realised that there would also be staff who were unaware of racist attitudes in their pupils. Even if they recognised examples of racism, they would be reluctant or unsure of how to deal with it. They would not have had the opportunity to reflect on their own reactions, or on the effects of an ethnocentric curriculum in creating or perpetuating such attitudes.

We were coming to the conclusion that we had to raise the basic issues involved with the whole staff before we could progress further or encourage any curriculum developments.

Initially a form of Racism Awareness Training organised by outsiders was considered. However, most courses were of at least two days' duration and would involve eight or nine teachers over a weekend, which in the current climate would only attract the most committed of staff. Training at any other time raised the problem of supply cover, which was ruled out before the issue of selection for such a course could be discussed.

We also noted the increasing criticisms of RAT, both theoretical and practical, which suggested that despite participants' individual changes and commitment to combat personal and institutional racism, little change had resulted when these individuals returned to their institutions.

An alternative is that advocated by John Twitchin (1985) in the use of an outsider to start things off. One difficulty with this is that teachers do not always take kindly to such people because 'they don't know the school, the pupils, the community or how I teach my subject'. Their presence is sometimes interpreted as an accusation that the staff are not doing their job properly and so, no matter how qualified or experienced, they may meet a resistance which can hinder or even block further individual or school development.

After several months deliberation the working party had decided that:

1 Further legitismation for our work was necessary.

2 We had to present multicultural education in all-white schools as 'good education' and an extension of professional expertise.

3 In order to place the issue firmly on the agenda of the whole school, the members of the working party had to raise the issue with the staff in a non-confrontational way.

After lengthy negotiations the Head agreed to an afternoon school closure, which gave us no more than two hours in which to raise the issue with the whole staff.

The working party then began a detailed consideration of the best way to use this short time. One idea that was considered and rejected, at this particular stage, was an examination of National Front youth magazines. It was felt that this immediately set racism within the context of extreme right-wing fanatics and would easily be dismissed. What we sought was material which would make staff see racism as an existing problem within the pupils and the school.

In the end we decided on small group work and a combination of strategies. One strategy was suggested by John Twitchin, with groups working on definitions of prejudice and racism. Another was to be a written collection of pupils' views on ethnic minorities expressed in class and youth club. The latter was suggested by Chris Gaine and produced very similar results to those described by Win Mould (1986).

As we knew this material would be seen by the staff, we were careful in how it was collected. Pupils of different ages were asked in a variety of lessons from Humanities to Science, and by some staff not on the working party, to write down their opinions on a variety of topics (not problems) of which the subject of ethnic minorities was just one. The percentage of negative or hostile remarks was also very similar to that quoted by Win Mould.

We also issued a questionnaire to staff on multicultural education and racism, which revealed a significant number of potential sympathisers as well as many who considered multicultural education as irrelevant to their subjects and own personal needs. This questionnaire did enable us to gauge the feelings and knowledge of the staff and to predict some likely responses to the afternoon's work.

The initial flurry of activity had brought our work in school to the attention of advisers and the Deputy Head was asked to join Hampshire's County Working Party to assist in formulating Hampshire's Policy on Multicultural Education. The school was also asked to provide two staff to participate in and one member of staff to tutor on a DES course on 'Curriculum for Ethnic Diversity', aimed at schools with few or no children of ethnic minority origin.

Having gained some legitimisation for our work and decided on the content of the afternoon, we attempted to structure the session and the use of the materials in a very detailed way because of the restrictions of time.

We decided that staff should work in cross-curricular groups, with a member of the working party in each group. Each working party member was given a pack containing detailed instructions, the format structure and timing of group work. The pack also contained a selection of the questions and comments which we expected would be raised, along with suggestions as to how they might be answered.

The group work consisted of a brainstorming session on ideas surrounding 'prejudice' and an attempt to arrive at an agreed definition. This was partly a warm-up exercise to a much longer examination of the meaning of racism. It was during these discussions that pupils' views and other material was included, to ensure relevance to our school and area and also to avoid personal confrontations. We were naturally aware that we had to work with our colleagues the next day and that an accusatory stance could prove counter-productive. Groups were not expected to reach an agreed definition on the meaning of racism but rather to have the opportunity to voice opinions, anxieties, experiences and to begin consideration of the part all-white schools play in contributing to the existing system of power-relations which serve to disadvantage certain ethnic groups in society.

Groups then reported back in a plenary session led by a member of the working party, whose task was to draw together points of agreement and concern. What emerged during this session was that, despite careful planning, some confrontations had occurred in one or two groups, while other groups had proceeded at considerable pace and arrived at some definite proposals. Members of the working party did occasionally find it difficult to handle such sensitive issues among colleagues, especially as the discussions sometimes remained tentative and vague with few definite conclusions.

The reporting back produced the following:

1 Genuine surprise and horror at the racism of pupils;

2 The possibility of a school policy on expressions of racism;

3 Requests for guidance on developing a more multicultural curriculum;

4 That the issue of sexism also be addressed;

5 A confusion over terminology, particularly use of words such as 'black' and 'tolerance';

6 Some staff still saw it all as irrelevant to them and the school.

The session was closed by the Head, who made it clear that the issue was now firmly on the school's agenda.

As these points had emerged from the staff themselves, the working party could build on them. After several discussions, it was decided that any further in-service work of an attitudinal type would prove counter-productive both personally and professionally. We had to accept that people change at different speeds and it would be more profitable to build on the positive than the negative.

Accordingly, we developed a two-pronged approach. Firstly, the working party would investigate several schools' anti-racist or multicultural policy statements and then draw up a policy statement suitable for our school. Secondly, we would seek further in-service time, which would be devoted partly to clarifying terminology and the handling of racist incidents, but predominantly to how to recognise ethnocentricism and how to develop and incorporate anti-racist multicultural perspectives in subject areas.

The process of change we were adopting was both 'top–down' and 'bottom–up', with the emphasis initially being on working with staff to identify, recognise and then suggest methods of change.

As the working party began examining various school policy statements, it also issued a report to all staff on what it was planning and included shortened extracts from articles on terminology and the limitations of a mono-cultural curriculum.

In examining school policy statements, we were initially struck by their language. This consisted of undoubtedly relevant and sometimes precise educational jargon – but who were these statements for? Staff, pupils or parents? It was quickly decided that any school policy statement should remain as accessible as possible to pupils and parents. Therefore, educational jargon had to be kept to a minimum.

The working party then decided on the areas which any policy statement should cover. These would include the ethos of the school, curriculum, racial abuse, language issues, staffing and, as a community school, links with the work of the Youth and Community activities.

The working party appointed two members to write the document and some in-service time was given to these staff. A first draft was prepared which was then examined and criticised constructively, resulting in a far more positive second version. This presented anti-racist multicultural education as an extension of existing practice in the school (see Appendix 1).

The second draft was primarily for staff, as it dealt in some detail with the nature of a multicultural curriculum and how racist incidents might be dealt with. It was envisaged that a shorter version would be prepared for parents.

The document was then circulated to staff several days before a scheduled staff meeting. Accompanying the policy statement was a sheet which briefly explained the evolution of the working party's thinking and gave space for staff to comment in writing on the separate sections of the policy statement. We recognised that some staff would either not be present at the meeting, or, for a variety of reasons, not speak or raise questions at a full staff meeting. It was essential that they were given a means through which they could communicate their feelings.

At the staff meeting it was stressed that this was a 'discussion' document and no final decision had been taken. What surprised members of the working party was that there were no negative responses, either to the need for such a policy or to its content, as there had been during the afternoon in-service session. Undoubtedly there were several factors which could explain this:

1 There had been a gap of several months between the in-service session on awareness and the drafting of a policy document. During that time many people had begun to question their personal and curriculum assumptions.

2 An article had appeared in *Multicultural Teaching* which explained the theoretical basis of the in-service session and strategy. That edition of the journal was devoted to all-white schools and featured developments underway in many parts of the country, (see Massey, 1987).

3 Some staff may have felt that 'it was going to happen anyway' and so withdrew from any involvement; but at least they had been given an open, democratic opportunity to be involved.

4 There may have been factors outside the school which influenced perception of the issue. The media presentation of anti-racism as the radical, totalitarian political ideology with no educational value had been thrown into doubt by the HMI positive report on Brent schools, which was widely reported on television, in the press and educational world.

There was a noticeably conciliatory tone from a colleague who had had a difficult time in his particular group during the in-service afternoon, and who later appeared quite hostile to developments along anti-racist multicultural lines. This time, there were requests for more information and guidance on curriculum issues.

As a result of the meeting, it was obvious that the working party would need to make few changes to the document in order for it to become a corner-stone of the school's educational philosophy.

The situation regarding the governors had also been raised and initially it was agreed that the document should be presented to them at a meeting. However, pressure of business indicated that the document would 'only be given a few minutes for both presentation and discussion'. Accordingly, we asked that the document be given more time at the next governors' meeting, which would not be for a few more months.

The second prong of our approach was to seek further in-service time in order to allow departments to examine alternative resources and develop their own multicultural and anti-racist approach. The newly appointed adviser for multicultural education proved useful in helping to provide legitimate support for our requests.

Initially the working party asked for two days, aware of how much time people often needed to come to terms with the issue and to see a positive way forward. Through negotiation this was reduced to one day, with a promise of further time to follow during the Autumn term. Taking full advantage of the change in funding arrangements for teachers' in-service education and the introduction of the Baker contract of employment for teachers, with its built-in in-service conditions, we were able to secure a whole day's closure.

As Frogmore is designated a community school, the working party extended the invitation to attend to youth and community workers, representatives of the governing body and ancilliary staff. We would have liked to include more parents at this stage, but it was felt that too large and diverse an audience would inhibit speakers and the work done in smaller groups. The priority at this stage had to be with the staff.

Having already established the need for staff development, as described above, all we had to do was to structure the day effectively and invite the speakers we already had in mind. The working party also felt that as this was to be a major impetus to the school's development and the first such attempt in the county, it should be evaluated; all participants having an opportunity to express their opinions on the speakers and their sessions, and on how they felt it all related to their own experience and subjects. In addition to this, we decided to try to overcome some of the confusion over terminology by distributing sheets of definitions published by Og Thomas and Rob Evans (1987). To avoid staff being given several loose-leaf sheets, we incorporated everything into a handbook, which was distributed to staff several days before the in-service day, and included all of the above together with an introduction and programme, cross-curricular groups and a brief history of multicultural developments in schools and in the county. The only major disappointment in the planning stage was the fact that the Head of the school was unable to be present, due to a term's secondment with IBM, and the chairman of the governors' last minute withdrawal for business reasons.

As we were going to be dealing with curricular issues and negative images, we arranged for a display of books, provided by Hampshire Library Services, on multicultural matters to be on display for several days in the reception area of the school. Berkshire Library Service also provided alternative resources on the day in a variety of subject areas.

Both the main speakers were briefed thoroughly by letter. Later, a meeting was arranged with both of them to discuss their approaches and links between the two main sessions. The adviser, having agreed to introduce and set the context of the day, was kept fully informed.

For the session on 'Handling Racist Incidents' the working party offered a selection of incidents that members had been made aware of for inclusion by the speaker, who agreed to use them without revealing their origin until later. The link between this and the following session on 'Bias and Omission in Resources' was to be the way in which curriculum materials in use may promote, sometimes unintentionally, views of other cultures which are inaccurate, negative and ethnocentric, resulting in the kind of attitudes displayed in the examples from the first session. Both sessions would include small cross-curricular activities and opportunities for discussion. The afternoon was to establish the point that curriculum development was already underway in two apparently contrasting areas of the school's curriculum: Humanities and Mathematics. Departments or faculties were then to be given a choice of four tasks to consider, and after an hour were to report back their deliberations and how they proposed to develop a more multicultural approach. The choices given were:

1 Select a frequently used resource book or work booklet.

a) Use the checklist provided to analyse the resource.

b) In the light of this, plan your course of action.

2 Select one part of your curriculum – topic, unit etc. and examine and modify, where necessary, the content and approaches used. If possible, identify any new resource.

3 Consider and plan ways in which cross-curricular links could foster the development of your work.

4 Plan the way a newly identified resource could be included in your curriculum.

The reporting back session would be chaired by the acting Headmaster, who would also request written proposals to be submitted over the next few days.

In the first full session, the speaker outlined with humorous exasperation examples of the racial abuse a black in-service provider still receives on visiting certain types of schools and, sometimes, in everyday life situations. She outlined why it was more serious and more hurtful to the victim and perpetrator than abuse over size, sight or region, and how it felt to be on the receiving end. This caused certain signs of discomfort amongst an all-white audience, and she began to be interrupted with questions about the true intentions of insults, i.e. harmless fun? She then distributed a photocopy of a piece of a pupil's work, which contained a list of 'dos' and 'don'ts' for a new settlement of human beings, including the statements: 'No coons', 'No pakis', 'No homosexuals', 'No teachers'. She asked people in pairs to discuss how they would react and then handle this situation. Finally, she asked what messages their chosen reaction would 'give to other pupils, black and white, and to parents'. Throughout this stage there was an attempt by some teachers to argue that this was the parents' responsibility and that we must be careful not to over-react, 'blow things up out of all proportion', or alienate parents. The speaker emphasised the power and autonomy a teacher has in a classroom, which is used to control other forms of offensive behaviour. She did not provide any definite solution on how such matters should be handled, but suggested that this was something we as individuals and as a school had to resolve. To aid us, she distributed a sheet of guidelines on handling racist incidents, produced in Berkshire.

The second full session, on 'bias and omission' seemed to produce an immediate negative and hostile response. Within a few minutes she was being challenged from the floor. 'But that's not racist!', 'How do you know that?' were typical of the interruptions. These continued hindering the development of her points. When staff were broken down into smaller groups to examine books following a checklist, the atmosphere was a lot more positive.

There may be several reasons for the reaction given by some to this session:

1 The manner of presentation may have been too assertive and examples of bias and omission occasionally too subtle.

2 The negative reaction of some senior male staff to an assertive female may relate more to issues of gender than the content of the session on ethnocentric bias.

3 Many of those who continually raised objections were senior staff in terms of age, experience or status within the school. The session was challenging, although we had planned for it to be fairly gentle, the assumptions and knowledge on which a substantial part of their personal and professional lives had been built.

As a result of this, and despite more positive feedback after small group work, the speaker did not have sufficient time to complete her intended tasks and give examples which were in use in our own school.

For the afternoon session, staff seemed much more relaxed. Here were two colleagues simply explaining what they were doing in their subject areas and why. Both were well received and hardly interrupted.

The tasks were then given to the staff for them to work on in their department or faculty with clear instructions as to what was expected at the end. This will be dealt with later.

Out of an anticipated return of 50, 35 people returned their evaluation sheets. Not all of the 35 attended all the sessions, due to other commitments, some missing one session and returning later. An analysis of the returns for the session on racist incidents showed the results in Figure 4. Clearly, of those returning the evaluation sheets, an overwhelming majority found the session valuable, although many were still uncertain about handling such incidents. This is hardly surprising, as for most of the staff it was not dealt with in their initial teacher training and they were only just becoming sensitised to the

	Agree strongly	Agree	Neutral	Disagree	Disagree strongly
The session on handling racist incidents was valuable.	11	11	1	3	
I now feel more confident in dealing with incidents.	3	13	7	3	
It would be useful if the school did have a public policy on such matters.	13	8	4		1

Figure 4 *Evaluation of session on racist incidents*

issue. However, what does emerge quite clearly from staff is the need for a school policy on the matter.

All those attending were encouraged not only to tick a few boxes, but also to write comments, which, it was hoped, would reflect their thinking. Examples of comments were:

It was very moving to hear racist incidents spoken about from a personal angle. I feel it is essential for the school to have a public policy which every member of staff should uphold.

I thought the speaker was excellent and maintained the right approach. I found the session reassuring, but I don't think it gave me any answers (are there any?)

It is vital that racist incidents are not dealt with in insolation and treated as one-offs. There should be a constant and ongoing policy that is clear to both staff and students, namely racist incidents and attitudes will not be tolerated and this is an intrinsic part of the school policy.

I found the practical advice very helpful. I feel there definitely needs to be a school policy on this matter.

I thought the session of great value, but this should be continued on a regular basis.

Some of those who disagreed made their points in the following ways:

All that was said was secondary to my concern. When I hear a racist comment I can't bring the issue up again in a Chemistry lesson.

I felt that many pertinent issues were ignored and basic educational principles undermined. I feel strongly that education is about teaching pupils to make decisions based upon balanced factual evidence. If this information is not given and the incident merely punished the problem is deferred to the playground, where it is infinitely more difficult to tackle.

Perhaps the feelings of most people are summed up in this final comment:

I was impressed by the courage of the speaker to express clearly and frankly what had happened to her. I liked the fact that she was uncompromising – I came away feeling invigorated although still not sure about my ability to deal with racist incidents effectively.

The second evaluation sheet was not quite so straightforward (see Figure 5). What was surprising was the number of people not just ticking the 'agree' column for the bias and omission session, but ticking the 'strongly agree' column. This was contrary to the impression being given at the time. There were obviously certain factors which allowed the impression to develop, as outlined previously, along with the inhibiting effect that a hierarchical structure in an organisation can have on people's confidence and ideas. The realisation of this situation was in itself a major benefit of the in-service day, although an unintentional one.

Some of the comments were very instructive, as they were not confined to the content of the session:

Unfortunately this session was hindered by the general attitude of the 'audience'. When bad manners prevail the message gets misunderstood and misinterpreted.

	Agree strongly	Agree	Neutral	Disagree	Disagree strongly
The session on bias and omission was valuable.	8	9	4	2	1
Head of Humanities' input was valuable.	4	15	3		
Mathematics teacher's input was valuable.	6	13	3		

Figure 5 *Evaluation of session on bias and omission*

The session went too far beyond what some people in the room could comprehend about racism. I think the staff need to look at their own racism first.

Defensive attitudes tended to be displayed in an aggressive way.

Others stuck to evaluating the session in general:

It was very useful to have the opportunity to examine books and rethink one's approach to selecting them.

Interesting to look at books in a new light; previously oblivious to how biased some of our everyday literature is.

While some staff agreed that it was a useful session, they did comment that:

Some of her examples were very extreme to the point of being ridiculous.

She was not realistic in some of her comments.

However, there were comments which highlighted matters that the working party had been concerned about in doing so much in one day, and which were compounded by the way in which the session developed. For example:

I still lack confidence in being able to recognise indirect racist texts.

... it was much too short. I was left feeling confused – many thoughts in the head but all jumbled.

It was unfortunate that some staff were left in this state and that no time was left to clarify or alleviate their anxieties, but it was something which we could return to during further in-service time and in different circumstances.

Of the three who disagreed or disagreed strongly on the value of the session, no-one gave any comment as to why.

It was encouraging to see that the two members of the staff who had volunteered to talk about developments in their subject areas were so positively received and, it is hoped, did act as a catalyst, showing that it can be done. After departments and faculties had met for an hour, they reported back to the acting Head: some in considerable detail, some in a tokenistic way; some being very innovative, and some finding great difficulty. All were worthy of support and encouragement.

This style of evaluation enabled the working party to plan each subsequent stage with more accuracy.

The draft school policy was circulated with a form on which staff could write comments, as we were aware that many staff, especially younger ones, did not always feel confident to air their thoughts and feelings at an open staff meeting. Only a few were completed, but the opportunity had been given. These comments were duly noted.

The policy statement was then sent to outsiders for comment, including the adviser and a number of the Team for Racial Equality in Education (TREE) based at Bulmershe. Many of the comments were positive and only a few changes were made to the draft document as a result of this consultation. A final version was prepared and circulated to all staff to give an opportunity for last minute comments. An explanation sheet was included for new staff.

Accompanying this was an account of what the working party had done and was planning. This included seeking the allocation of two further INSET days to multicultural education to cover the areas of need revealed by the evaluation of the previous whole day's INSET. Although there had been previous incidents where a few individuals had voiced their anxieties, this was the first occasion on which there was a formal objection.

The Science Faculty did not object to multicultural initiatives, in fact it was already implementing change, but rather the time devoted to it. A statement was issued to all staff requesting that multi-culturalism now take a back seat to GCSE implementation and accusing the working party of not addressing expressed needs of staff.

This was felt by the working party to be a misrepresentation of what had happened in the past and a lack of any clear appreciation that anti-racist multicultural education had to underpin everything in the curriculum. This was especially relevant to GCSE criteria. These sentiments were made clear to the Science staff and others. There is no doubt that feelings among those involved were very strong, and the end of the Christmas term is not really conducive to cool, rational discussion. The dispute needed the intervention of the Head, who chaired what turned out to be an amicable discussion, where misunderstandings were rectified and apologies given and received. However, there was a clear statement in favour of the school's commitment to developing a multicultural perspective from the Head, but a negotiated compromise of one rather than two INSET days being devoted to this development was the result. Such meetings and compromises are obviously necessary in developing an anti-racist multicultural staff development programme and have to be allowed for in any planning process.

A meeting was also arranged with the school governors to present and discuss the school policy statement. At this meeting, the discussion occupied three times the amount of time originally allocated to it on the agenda. The presence of governors who had attended the INSET day was very effective, as they could describe what had happened and the positive effects it was having on the school and them personally.

Much of the discussion was taken up with the governors remarking on the relevance of this perspective in education to adult working life. In their roles as parents, employees and employers, they could appreciate the need for such an approach, and many expressed regret at not having been exposed to this during their own formal education, as many now worked in a multi-ethnic environment.

There was a certain concern that, although this was sound educationally and morally, 'we wouldn't go as far as Brent'. What was concerning some were the media images and distortions of anti-racism in ILEA which have left their mark not only on parents, but on teachers too. This had to be recognised and dealt with, by encouraging those who seemed anxious about 'the diluting British culture' or censorship to come into school, to take part in INSET themselves, and to see the enriching possibilities of anti-racist multicultural education.

Once these concerns had been dealt with, there was no hesitation by the governors in approving the policy statement.

With the support of the governors, the Head and the majority of staff there was no way in which anti-racist multicultural initiatives or those directly involved in their promotion could easily be marginalised. Consequently, the working party could plan with some confidence for further INSET.

This time notes went to faculty heads and house heads, giving them the opportunity to discuss with their staff how they would like to use the time during an INSET day.

One popular request was to work with teachers from other schools, particularly from multi-ethnic schools, who had implemented anti-racist multicultural approaches.

This proved too difficult to arrange for just one school, particularly at a time of GCSE implementation, as many schools felt they could not spare the personnel and there was, in any case, the problem of supply cover. However, there is no reason why this could not work in future, especially on a cluster or pyramid system, so that several schools would be involved.

Visits to other schools were also requested. This again proved difficult, but one school was prepared to co-operate fully. We were able to send a group of staff on a visit covering areas such as Creative Arts, Home economics, Humanities and the pastoral system. This visit was of considerable benefit to those involved in providing stimulating and legitimising insights into the kind of work which has become part and parcel of many teachers' professional expertise in multi-ethnic schools.

The INSET day was not just to focus on curriculum issues; time was also devoted to discussion of incidents of a racist nature. Prior to the day, staff were asked to submit examples of racist incidents which they were aware of. In the end, an edited collection was put together which covered examples of racist jokes in class, racially abusive behaviour on school trips and physical violence. All had occurred in this mainly white school in the previous three months.

Again staff discussed in cross-curricular groups how we should respond to such incidents. They then moved into house groups to discuss how this would affect discipline and counselling procedures in their house.

It resulted in a general call for further guidance for all staff on responding to racist incidents, which would not be prescriptive, but ensure a consistency of approach. It appeared that no member of staff would allow incidents to go unchallenged, but that they still lacked confidence in how they dealt with such events.

The rest of the day was devoted to staff working on an aspect of their curriculum of their own choosing. They worked in faculties or departments, but they set their own agenda.

Lunch was provided and was a mixture of 'traditional British' and Asian food. The latter was prepared by an Asian member of the community who taught evening classes. We decided that this could be used as a learning experience for ancillary staff in the kitchens and a Home Economics teacher, as they would all work together in preparing the food. Set in the context of the school's development, we also felt that it would not be tokenistic.

The meal also provided a very relaxed atmosphere in which staff were able to discuss matters which had arisen during the day at leisure.

At the end of the day, faculties and departments had to produce an account of what they had worked on and what they were planning for the future, which was available for the Head and others to examine.

	Agree strongly	Agree	Neutral	Disagree	Disagree strongly
The first session of the INSET day has enabled me to feel more confident in dealing with incidents in school.		10	10	3	
The time devoted to work on the curriculum was about right.	2	12	5	3	

Figure 6 *Evaluation of INSET day*

The evaluation of the day produced some very interesting replies, most of which were positive about the structure of the day and complimentary about the opportunity to talk with colleagues about how to respond to classroom situations. The food and atmosphere also received favourable comments. The feelings regarding racist incidents are summarised in Figure 6.

THE EFFECTS ON THE WHOLE SCHOOL

At Frogmore, the evaluation strategy has been to record all curricular developments as well as all other significant changes in the school. Over three years this has produced the following:

1 Curriculum development

Mathematics
Years 1 and 2 Rangoli patterns.
Year 2 Different number systems.

English
Year 3 Focus on texts by authors not native-born white British, e.g. Faroukh Dondy, *Come to Mecca*, poetry by Grace Nicholls, James Berry, John Agard; contact with Catalan-speaking pupils in Barcelona.
Years 4 and 5 Texts from a wide variety of folk traditions; discussion around texts confronting racial issues, e.g. Harper Lee, *To Kill a Mockingbird*; examination of texts by young people of diverse ethnic backgrounds living in Britain; investigation of dialect or non-standard forms of English.

Integrated Humanities
Years 1 and 2 Exploration Unit on contact with other cultures; Slavery Unit with texts from West Indies, featuring Toussaint l'Ouverture and Harriett Tubman in the USA; World Links Project; multi-faith work on sacred places and festivals; study of novels and poems that reflect a multicultural world and confront racism.

Biology
Year 3 Biotechnology – Egyptian brewing and baking; Syrian moulds; eastern fermented milk products; sugar cane production.
Years 5 and 6 Tissue culture; oil palms (Arabian); Japanese fuel cells; future plans to include animal cell tissue; American–Chinese Brassicae project.

Physics
Famous physicists (of any nationality) already commonly referred to; searching for new positive multicultural images; scope also in Science at Work modules, e.g. cosmetics, building science, food and microbes.

Modern Languages
Year 1 One group in each class allocated a French-speaking country, as opposed to a region in France; dispelling of national stereotypes; language taster days – opportunity to try Russian, Spanish, Chinese, Italian, Thai.

Art
Multiculturalism integrated into art department policy, especially in visual displays, design and techniques; permeates 4th and 5th year examination work.

Drama
Modular approach in 1st and 2nd year to include themes on different cultural perspectives and confronting issues of prejudice, discrimination, rejection in a variety of ways.

Home Economics
Food and nutrition course based on UNICEF pack; world cookery course – bringing in people from different cultural backgrounds to demonstrate and explain wherever possible.

PE/Dance
Displays covering the origin of sport; participation and personalities from Asia, America, Australasia, Europe; more dance workshops planned, e.g. African dance and Kathakali.

Geography
Year 3 Development Indicators Unit – Images and Stereotypes of the Third World.
Year 4 and 5 Inequality in Brazil; development of industry and urbanisation (rich v. poor, shanty towns etc.)
Year 6 Inequality in cities; progress in agriculture and industry; Option Module – Alternative Approaches to Development – measuring development gap, review of aid policies.

History
Year 4 and 5 Medicine through time – Arab, European contributions; work of Mary Seacole; Arab – Israeli crisis.

Learning for Life (PSE)

Use of Afro-Caribbean Education Resource pack, *Ourselves*, to assist in the process of growing up in a multicultural society; all units stress diversity, even in use of names for role play; unit on 'Work' includes a wider world perspective incorporated into Aims and Objectives.

Social Studies

All units stress diversity; 'Multicultural Britain' tackles common myths, the origins of prejudice and racism, the effects of racism and strategies to combat it.

Music

Year 1 Classical and folk music of India.
Year 3 Looking at 'Indipop'.
Year 4 Comparing Asian and Afro-Caribbean music.
Year 5 Survey of World Music (Peru, Kenya, Japan, Kashmir, Hungary, England); Choir and Orchestra – arrangements of Hungarian folksongs (inc. singing in Hungarian); African Drum Group; Recorder Group – doing Recorder Achievement Tests of Kenya Conservatoire of Music.

School Links

1989 Class link with No. 109 Middle School, Beijing (pre Tianamen Square June 1989).
1989 Class link with rural school in British Columbia, Canada.
1990 Class link with multi-ethnic school in Forest Gate, London.
1990 Two classes linked with school in Kenya.
1990 Developing links through Campus 2000 with schools in Germany and Japan with a view to using electronic mailing to exchange pupils' work.

2 Pastoral system

All racist incidents are dealt with immediately through referral system and treated seriously. This involves counselling and, where necessary, the school's disciplinary sanctions in accordance with the authority's guidelines (1990).

3 Pupil views

One of the main criticisms of Frogmore's developments is that pupils have not been systematically involved as recommended in the Burnage Report. Their awareness has mainly been through those few lessons dealing directly with racism and the role of all-white schools and, on occasions, through the pastoral system. One interesting example of pupil involvement in the all-white context is the 'pupil-speak' anti-racist school policy produced at Bohunt School, Liphook, Hampshire (Roberts and Massey, 1991). This offers a greater possibility for creating the sense of 'ownership' advocated by the Burnage Report.

In terms of the effect of the overall school developments, we were still in the early days of implementation and our evidence and evaluation is not as systematic or complete as we would like.

Firstly, we acknowledge that we have not eliminated racist attitudes in all our pupils. However, there are some indicators of change. The number of pupils with hard-core racist attitudes is noticeably smaller and their tendency to dominate class discussions has been tempered (a factor also noticed at Bohunt school). Those pupils with positive and anti-racist views now feel supported, not only by the teacher but also by the school, and tend to be more outspoken. This has a positive effect on others, in terms of being influenced away from racism, a message which is reinforced by the school as a whole.

Staff have also commented favourably on pupil reaction to some curriculum initiatives, especially in Mathematics and Home Economics. Some have noticed how there seems to be a greater knowledge and awareness among pupils of other cultures and their contributions alongside the negative images of black and Asian people in Britain and other parts of the world.

In a revised module on 'Multicultural Britain' in Social Studies, which dealt with immigration, discrimination, prejudice, racism and racial attacks using a variety of teaching methods, third years responded to the following two questions as part of an evaluation:

a) How would you describe your views about people from other cultures before these lessons?

b) Do you think any of the lessons have had any effect on your attitudes and/or knowledge about people from other cultures?

Pupil 1

a) Different, black people cause trouble, Indians smelling.

b) The experiment* the teacher done changed my views a lot.
   I don't judge people by their appearance.
   (*Refers to the film The Eye of the Storm)

Pupil 2

a) Well, my dad is virtually racist so I think that I had a pretty low opinion of them.

b) I think now that I will think twice before calling someone a racist name because it does hurt!

Pupil 3

a) My views on other cultures was plain I wasn't bothered about them and didn't take much notice of them.

b) Yes, before these lessons I didn't think much of racism but now I understand and I think the whole thing is wrong and will try to stop it.

Pupil 4

a) I don't think I was keen on people from other cultures before, and would not have had friends.

b) This lesson has changed me. I now know how they feel and am totally on their side now.

Pupil 5

a) I didn't realise they had such a rough deal. I didn't see them as primitive or that they were really different but deep down I think I might have had racist views.

b) Yes, I think they have. I'm sympathetic to black people now and I don't think I would laugh at jokes about them now.

Pupil 6

Well, I'd never go around calling people paki and stuff anyway, but I feel a lot more strongly about racism now than I did before.

Of the 80 pupils who completed this evaluation, only about 10 per cent said that their negative or racist views remained unchanged.

It is, of course, not simply these lessons which are responsible for the gradual shift in pupil attitudes and behaviour, but rather the fact that they now take place in an institution which positively values cultural diversity. This message is reinforced in curricular materials, visual displays and teachers' responses to expressions of racism.

4 School aims and objectives

These have recently been rewritten and contain the following statements:

To promote equality of opportunity and to correct bigotry, prejudice or any other form of discriminatory practice, particularly on the grounds of disability, sex or race. To prepare pupils for life in a multicultural society.

To offer teaching which reflects positively the various cultures of Britain and the rest of the world, and the contribution of other various cultures to all areas of human knowledge and experience.

To demonstrate an opposition to all forms of anti-social behaviour including prejudice, sexism and racism.

5 Presentation of policy to parents

Another criticism of Frogmore's progress regards the limited involvement of parents during the early stages of institutional change. It was not until the second stage of in-service training that parents were included in the planning process. Really parents need to be involved at the awareness-raising stage if their support and commitment is to be gained. This can be achieved through the existing parent organisations, using similar techniques to those used with teachers. The involvement of parent-governors was crucial in the development process but needed to be wider than that particular group.

From the second stage of staff training, many staff were aware of the need to address the issue of parents and their influence on the development of positive attitudes to cultural diversity. It has to be recognised, as Adorno (1954) pointed out, that an attitude has a function. At home it may be that a racist attitude helps the child to 'fit in' and be accepted in the family situation. For such a child, the conflicting value positions of the school and the home, and the dissonance thus created, tend to lead to the home 'winning', resulting in further alienation from school.

Consequently, the issue of parental involvement (which has often been an underlying anxiety for Heads of all-white schools) needs as much careful thought as staff in-service training. What follows is just one possible strategy.

It had been decided quite early on at Frogmore to raise parents' awareness in general through a process of 'subtle permeation', not least because of the tone of media coverage of these kinds of developments at that time. This would mean that new curriculum materials or topics and, where practical, those events which involve parents entering the school, such as parents' evenings, would reflect the growing anti-racist multicultural developments through displays of pupil work and other visual images. In an attempt directly to broaden parental knowledge of and involvement in the work, it was decided to focus initially on parents of first years. There were two reasons for this:

1 There is no school hall and so large-scale meetings of parents do not take place. Instead, meetings are usually on a year basis.

2 Following the in-service sessions, most departments had begun curricular developments in the lower school, especially the first year.

It was also decided to avoid any formal presentation of the policy. This can provide a platform for a few vocal dissenters to undermine the intentions of the school, often forcing the Head and others on to the defensive. It can also appear to be a very authoritarian form of policy making. The policy and the curricular developments needed to be seen as non-threatening and, most of all, as *good practice*. So, why not show them in action, as well as some of the results of anti-racist multicultural approaches?

It was agreed that we would hold an evening of curriculum workshops in July 1989, which would actively involve parents, pupils and teachers, sometimes with pupils teaching parents new skills. One of the best ways to get parents into school for an evening is, as many teachers know, to have their children involved in activities. Another factor which can affect attendance is the title given to an evening. An evening devoted to anti-racist multicultural education in an all-white area would, it was felt, attract only a handful of already committed parents or those forcefully opposed. The evening was therefore ambiguously titled, 'Workshops across the Curriculum', but this symbolically stated that anti-racist multicultural work was part of the mainstream curriculum. Some of the activities/workshops had a central anti-racist theme; others were more multicultural or international. Pupils' artwork, which had been specifically multicultural, was also on display, as were our international links through correspondence with schools in Canada and Beijing. The workshops held were:

Pupil-designed games and games from other cultures;

French throughout the world and role playing;

Literature and poetry readings;

IT and Campus 2000;

Different number systems;

Role play by sixth years on stereotyping and racism;

Chinese calligraphy;

Biotechnology;

Indian cookery.

The significant difference in this approach is that the policy is seen as practically rooted in the pupils' direct experience of the curriculum. All of the activities were what pupils had done, or were about to do as part of their educational experience at Frogmore.

As the working party continued the planning of this evening, the SMT realised that this was a potentially useful public relations exercise, so invitations were sent to parents of prospective first year pupils. After all, it was demonstrating good practice.

On the evening itself each workshop ran three times, so that parents had an opportunity to experience several activities. One of the most successful was the group of sixth years (all white) who performed the role play on stereotyping and racism, supported by two teachers. The role play of a racist incident was taken from the evidence we had collected from staff and set in a real classroom situation. The action was stopped at the same crucial point each time and the small audience was asked to discuss with the students (and teachers, if necessary) the following questions:

1 How should the teacher react?

2 What should the teacher do next?

3 What would be the consequences?

4 What messages do the pupils receive as a result?

Reactions from parents were often encouraging in terms of the seriousness with which they felt it should be treated. No-one who spoke argued that it should be ignored. Many also seemed pleased that teachers were giving such matters careful thought. For some parents it was obviously the first time that they had considered such a situation, and they were being forced to reflect on their attitudes.

What is significant about this, in terms of the effects of the management of change, is that:

1 A group of staff and students now had the confidence to confront and explore the issue of racism with parents.

2 The school's policy could be seen as necessary and relevant.

The evening ended very informally with parents, pupils and staff coming together for a selection of Indian food and drink cooked by first years in collaboration with an evening class of adults, led by a Muslim Adult Education Tutor, with whom the pupils had worked before. By this time all parents had a copy of a small booklet, which explained the background to our work in a local and national context and gave the school policy statement.

The general reaction to the evening from parents was favourable and supportive not only of the anti-racist multicultural approach but also of the format of the evening. They enjoyed seeing the work of their children as well as seeing them *at work* and sometimes learning from them.

	Agree strongly	Agree	Neutral	Disagree	Disagree strongly
I feel that my views on the relevance of multicultural education have become more favourable over time.	5	14	3	1	
I have found that the work on racism has made me more conscious of it outside school as well.	4	11	6	1	1

Figure 7 *Staff evaluation of complete INSET programme*

6 Feeder schools

One of the primary schools feeding Frogmore has become increasingly involved in multicultural initiatives through a school twinning project, which has led to some curriculum developments. It is now felt important that regular meetings are held with all feeder schools to discuss continuity of experience from 5 to 18 in relation to education for cultural diversity.

7 Staff views

As part of the evaluation of the in-service programme, we asked about changes in staff views towards multicultural education. After eighteen months development Figure 7 reveals that there were considerable professional and personal changes in staff perceptions.

SUMMARY

The experience outlined above of one all-white secondary school's attempt to come to terms with anti-racist multicultural education and the institutional changes needed shows that, if there is a sound understanding of how change can be managed at a personal and institutional level, the chances of success are improved.

The National Curriculum may offer opportunities which will serve to legitimise the need for this approach, especially in the all-white situation but, unless developments take place within a whole-school framework, an unco-ordinated tokenism will be the most likely outcome.

There is no reason why the greater emphasis now placed on continuity and progression in the National Curriculum cannot apply to anti-racist multicultural education. Whole-school developments can take place within a 'pyramid' or 'cluster' framework, and joint cross-phase working parties and INSET on anti-racist multicultural education can be held involving all the schools.

The Frogmore experience began before the days of the National Curriculum, LMS and the new ERA. However, the process of developing and managing change within an institution remains broadly the same. There are lessons which can be learned from Frogmore. Many of these have already been pointed out, such as the involvement of governors in INSET, the manner of raising parental awareness, and the need to involve pupils at an earlier stage. These strategies are not just applicable to all-white schools but can be effective in other school contexts.

Monitoring and evaluation are also issues which need careful consideration in any school in the 1990s, and the development of performance indicators should be of great assistance in evaluating an institution's development.

A commitment to countering racial injustice is, of course, necessary to carry out this kind of development. But that in itself is not sufficient. An understanding of how racism is perpetuated through a society's political and cultural institutions, as well as a familiarity with the mechanics of personal and institutional change, are also prerequisites. It is to this process that this book has aimed to contribute.

Figure 8 (shown overleaf) links the developments at Frogmore Community School with the model outlined in Figure 3 in Chapter 5. It is not a straightforward linear model, as certain stages, such as those associated with staff training, will recur. The boxed sections are those which form essential elements of a staff-development programme.

Stage	Development
1	Dissemination of Swann, county policy, NCC documents, DES statements.
2	Gaining support from Inspectors, Head; identifying allies; staff and curriculum meetings.
3	Forming working party; setting aims; collecting evidence.
4	Visiting other schools; examining policies etc.; INSET for individuals.
5	Staff survey: knowledge, skills, attitudes; looking at curriculum; pupil views.

6 | Awareness raising; school-based INSET; defining terms: prejudice, racism; pupil views; role of school: curriculum, staff; evaluation.

Feedback: all staff; time and space for reflection.

School-based INSET.
Knowledge: national and local; cultural pluralism today and in the past.
Skills: listening to black people; recognising bias.
Target-setting for departments; evaluation.

6/7	Feedback to all staff; negotiating policy statement.
6/7/8	Experiential; visiting other schools/teachers; staff discussion of policy.
7/8	Presentation to governors; endorsement; communication to staff; future planning.

8 | Developing competence in responding to racist incidents; whole-school approach; curriculum development; evaluation.

| 9 | Feedback to staff; encouraging permeation, cross-curricular links; pupil involvement, acceptance, commitment; parental involvement; wider community; employers. |
| 10 | Implementations; evaluation; developing performance indicators. |

Figure 8 *Staff-development programme of Frogmore Community School*

Appendix

FROGMORE COMMUNITY SCHOOL

Our approach to multicultural education

We are a school which has pupils from a range of cultural backgrounds. For some time now we have been developing a more multicultural approach to our teaching and this has been endorsed by the Swann Report and Hampshire's own policy.

We firmly believe that a multicultural approach to education is the basis of a 'good education' for all pupils.

Because of our situation we recognise that putting multicultural ideas into practice is difficult. It may involve examining our own prejudices or searching more carefully for relevant materials. It may also mean becoming more sensitive to perspectives of the world other than our own. However, we must remember that the school is part of a multicultural society and pupils will live and work in a world in which they come into contact with people from many cultures.

Aims

We believe that a school should aim:

1 To prepare all pupils for life in a multicultural society.

2 To offer teaching which reflects positively the various cultures of Britain and the contribution of other cultures to all areas of human knowledge and experience.

3 To demonstrate an opposition to and combat all forms of prejudice and racism.

Ethos and atmosphere

A school committed to such aims should reflect this in the way it treats and values all pupils. It should also guide everyday practices such as the correct spelling and pronunciation of names.

Visual displays in the school should wherever possible reflect and celebrate the cultural diversity of Britain.

Teaching content and method

A prime cause of prejudice is ignorance and misunderstanding, and racism can be exhibited in the way knowledge is presented to pupils. This can be countered by a conscious determination to take account of the contributions of other cultures and races to human knowledge and experience, which has often been under-estimated or ignored. Teaching content or method should therefore seek to:

1 Create an understanding of and interest in different environments, societies, systems and cultures across the world.

2 Study the reasons for the patterns of racism and inequality in this country and the world.

3 Inform and encourage pupils to analyse and recognise that each society has its own values, traditions and everyday living patterns which should be considered in the context of that society.

4 Actively value the contributions made to human knowledge by cultures and countries outside the western world.

5 Explore the ideas and opinions which emerge from particular cutlural experiences.

6 Ensure that where possible all teaching resources are multicultural and contain positive images of people from ethnic minority groups.

Racial abuse

Racism can be expressed in a variety of forms, such as:

Physical attacks
Verbal abuse – including name-calling and racist jokes
Intimidation
Racist literature and symbols
Refusal to co-operate with people because of their ethnic group
Racist graffiti
Negative images in books and materials

As with any unacceptable behaviour, racist behaviour should be dealt with through the school's established disciplinary procedures. Words or phrases which serve to denigrate a whole culture or ethnic group should not be tolerated.

However, the manner in which staff respond will depend on the situation. In minor incidents an indication that such expressions are offensive may suffice. Staff have a duty to explain to offenders why their behaviour or language is unacceptable.

It is only persistent offenders or violent incidents which should be referred immediately to Faculty, House or Senior Staff. Only in the most serious of cases would this result in the employment of the severest of the school's disciplinary sanctions.

Youth and Community

The Youth and Community Department forms an integral part of the Community School provision. In all activities it is committed to equal opportunities and places emphasis on educating young people to have an understanding of a multicultural, multi-ethnic community.

Staffing

Greater cultural diversity amongst the staff should be seen as a desirable development.

All future appointments should include in the criteria for selection a knowledge of and a commitment to the stated aims of the school.

Staff should monitor their own conduct and language in regard to this matter and under no circumstances should they appear to condone racist usage.

Encouragement should be given to staff who seek to broaden their professional expertise through in-service courses and establishing closer links with ethnic minority groups.

Language

Pupils' languages are a rich resource to the school and community. Pupils who speak more than one language should have their bilingualism valued. They should feel confident to speak, hear and read their own language. Bilingual pupils might need additional support in certain situations. Therefore, appropriate materials and strategies should be developed.

Bibliography

ABBOT, B.; GILBERT, S. AND LAWSON, R. (1989) Towards anti-racist awareness: confessions of some teacher converts, in P. WOODS (ed.) *Working for Teacher Development Dereham*. Peter Francis.

ADORNO, T. W. (ed.) (1950) *The Authoritarian Personality*. New York: Harper & Row.

ALLPORT, G. (1958) *The Nature of Prejudice*. New York, Doubleday, Anchor.

ANDERSON, B. (1989) Education and Anti-racism: Strategies of the 1990s, *Multicultural Teaching* 7, 3.

ANTONOURIS, G. and RICHARDS, J. K. (1985) *Race in Education*. Trent Polytechnic.

BALL, W. and TROYNA, B (1989) Dawn of a New Era? The Education Reform Act, 'Race' and LEA's, *Education Management and Administration*.

BANKS, J. A.; CORTES, L. E.; GAY, G.; GARCIA, R. L. and OCHOA, A. S. (1976) *Curriculum Guidelines for Multi-ethnic Education*. Washington D. C.: Nelson Council for Social Studies.

BANKS, J. A. (1981) *Multi-ethnic Education: Theory and Practice* (1st ed.) Boston: Allyn and Bacon.

BANKS, J. A. (1986) *Multicultural Education: Development Paradigms and Goals*, in BANKS, J. A. and LYNCH, J. (eds). *Multicultural Education in Western Societies*. London: Holt, Rinehart and Winston.

BANKS, J. A. (1988) *Multi-ethnic Education: Theory and Practice* (2nd ed.). Boston: Allyn and Bacon.

BANKS, J. A. (forthcoming) Education for Cultural Diversity: Historical and Contemporary Developments in the USA, in FYFE, A. and FIGUEROA, P. (eds) *Education for Cultural Diversity*. Basingstoke: Macmillan.

BANKS, J. A. and BANKS MCKEE C. A. (1989) *Multicultural Education:*

Issues and Perspectives. Boston, Allyn and Bacon.

BARKER, M. (1981) *The New Racism*. London: Junction Books.

BENTON, M. (1985) Rat Back to the Drawing Board, *New Community*, Summer.

BEN-TOVIN, G. *et al.* (1982) A Political Analysis of Race in the 1980s, in HUSBAND (ed.) *Race in Britain: Continuity and Change*. London: Hutchinson.

BIRLEY HIGH SCHOOL (1980) *Multicultural Education in the 1980s*: The report of a Working Party of Teachers at Birley High School. Manchester: City of Manchester Education Committee.

BERKSHIRE LEA (1983) *Education for Racial Equality*: Policy Paper 1. Reading Education Department.

BOSTON, L. T. (1988) *Race, Class and Conservation*. Winchester, Mass: Unwin.

BRANDT, G. (1986) *The Realisation of Antiracist Teaching*. Lewes: Falmer Press.

BRITTAIN, E. (1976) Multi-racial Education 2: Teacher Opinion on Aspects of School Education, *Research* **18**, 3.

BROWN, C. (1984) *Black and White Britain: The Third PSI Survey*. London: Heineman.

BULLIVANT, B. M. (1981) *The Pluralist Dilemma in Education*. Sydney: Allen and Unwin.

BULLIVANT, B. M. (1984) Pluralism, Cultural Maintenance and Evolution, *Multilingual Matters*. Clevedon, Avon.

BURROWS, D. (1985) From a Different Perspective, *Times Educational Supplement*, 12 April.

BURTONWOOD, N. (1986) Inset and Multicultural/Anti-Racist Education, *British Journal of Inservice* **13**, 1.

CARBY, H. V. (1982) *Schooling in Babylon, The Empire Strikes Back*. London: Hutchinson.

CARRINGTON, B.; CHIVERS, T. and WILLIAMS, T. Grenber, Leisure, Sport: A Case Study of Young People of South Asian descent, *Leisure Studies* **6**, 3.

CARRINGTON, B. and SHORT, G. (1989a) *Race in the Primary School*. Windsor: NFER Nelson.

CARRINGTON, B. and SHORT, G. (1989b) Policy or Presentation? The Psychology of Antiracist Education, *New Community*, **15**, 2, 227–40.

CARTER, T. (1985) Working within the Power Structures in the Quest for Change, *Multicultural Teaching*, 3, 3.

CARTER, B. and WILLIAMS, J. (1987) Attacking Racism in Education, in TROYNA, B. (ed.) *Racial Inequality in Education*. London: Tavistock.

CHIN, R. and BENNE, K. D. (1976) General Strategies for Effecting Change in Human Systems, in CHIN, R. and BENNE, K. D. (eds) *The Planning of Change*, (3rd Edition).

COCHRANE, R. and BILLIG, M. (1984) I'm not National Front Myself, but . . ., *New Society*, 17 May.

COMMISSION FOR RACIAL EQUALITY (1988) *Learning in Terror*.

CONNOR, W. (1971) Nations Building and Nations Developing, *World Studies* No. 24.

COARD, B. (1971) *How the West Indian Child is Made Educationally Subnormal in the British School System*. London: New Beacon Books.

COHEN, L. and MANION, L. *Multicultural Classrooms*. London: Croom Helm.

COLE, M. (1986) Multicultural Education and The Politics of Racism in Britain, *Multicultural Teaching* **5**, 1.

COMER, T. (1984) *Education in Multicultural Societies*. London: Croom Helm.

COMER, J. and JONES, L. (eds) (1972) White Racism – Its Roots, Form, Function, *Black Psychology*. New York: Harper Row.

COMMITTEE OF INQUIRY NTO THE EDUCATION OF CHILDREN FROM ETHNIC MINORITY GROUPS (Rampton Committee) (1981). *West Indian Childen in our Schools* (Interim report). London: HMSO.

COMMONWEALTH IMMIGRANTS ADVISORY COUNCIL (1964) 2nd Report. London: HMSO.

CRAFT, M. (ed.) (1981) *Teaching in a Multicultural Society: The Task for Teacher Education*. London: Falmer Press.

CRAFT, M. (ed.) (1984) *Education for Diversity*. London: Falmer Press.

CRAFT, A. and KLEIN, G. (1986) *Agenda for Multicultural Teaching* SCDC. York: Longman.

DANIEL, N. W. (1968) *Racial Discrimination in England*. Harmondsworth: Penguin.

DAVEY, A. (1983) *Learning to be Prejudiced: Growing up in Multi-Ethnic Britain*. London: Edward Arnold.

DAVID, J. (1982) *School Based Strategies: Implications for Government Policies*. Minnesota: Bay Area Research Group.

DEPARTMENT OF EDUCATION AND SCIENCE (1963) *English for Immigrants* (Pamphlet 43). London: HMSO.

DEPARTMENT OF EDUCATION AND SCIENCE (1965) *The Education of*

Immigrants, Circular 7/65. London: HMSO.

DEPARTMENT OF EDUCATION AND SCIENCE (1971) *The Education of Immigrants* (Education Survey No. 13). London: HMSO.

DEPARTMENT OF EDUCATION AND SCIENCE (1977) *Education in Schools: A Consultative Document* (Green Paper, Cmnd 6869). London: HMSO.

DEPARTMENT OF EDUCATION AND SCIENCE (1989a) *National Curriculum, From Policy to Practice*. London: HMSO.

DEPARTMENT OF EDUCATION AND SCIENCE (1989b) *The Education Reform Act 1988* (Circular 5/89). London: HMSO.

DEPARTMENT OF EDUCATION AND SCIENCE/NATIONAL CURRICULUM COUNCIL (1988a) *English 5–16*. London: HMSO.

DEPARTMENT OF EDUCATION AND SCIENCE/NATIONAL CURRICULUM COUNCIL (1988b) *Science 5–16*. London: HMSO.

DEPARTMENT OF EDUCATION AND SCIENCE/NATIONAL CURRICULUM COUNCIL (1989a) *Design and Technology*. London: HMSO.

DEPARTMENT OF EDUCATION AND SCIENCE/NATIONAL CURRICULUM COUNCIL (1989B) *Geography 5–16*. London: HMSO.

DEPARTMENT OF EDUCATION AND SCIENCE/NATIONAL CURRICULUM COUNCIL (1990) *History* (Final Report). London: HMSO.

DU BOIS, W. E. B. (1920) *Darkwater*. New York: Harcourt, Brace and Horne.

DUMMETT, A. (1986), RAT, ART or What?, *New Society*, 10 October.

DUNCAN, C. (1986) Towards a Multicultural Curriculum – Secondary, in ARORA, R. and DUNCAN, C. (eds) *Multi-cultural Education: Towards Good Practice*. London: Routledge and Kegan Paul.

EDELMAN, M. (1964) *The Symbolic Uses of Politics*. Urbana: University of Illinois Press.

EDWARDS, A. D. (1976) *Language in Culture and Class*. London: Heineman.

EGGLESTON, J. (1986) *The Educational, Vocational Experience of 15–18 Year Old Young People of Minority Ethnic Groups*. Coventry: University of Warwick, Department of Education.

EGGLESTON, J. (1988) The New Education Bill and Assessment: Some Implications for Black Children, *Multicultural Teaching*, 6, 2.

FIGUEROA, P. M. E. (1984) Race Relations and Cultural Differences: Some Ideas on a Racial Frame of Reference, in VERMA, K. and BAGLEY, L. (eds) *Race Relations and Cultural Differences*. London: Croom Helm.

FIRTH, R. (1958) *Human Types*. New York: Mentor.

FLEW, A. (1986) Education against Racism, in O'KEEFE, D. (ed.) *The Wayward Curriculum*. London: Social Affairs Unit.

FLEW, A. (1987) *Power to the Parents*. London: Sherwood Press.

FLUDE, M. (1974) Sociological Accounts of Differential Educational Attainment in M. FLUKE and J. AKIER (eds) *Educability, Schools and Ideology*. London: Croom Helm.

FOOT, P. (1965) *Immigration and Race in British Politics*. Harmondsworth: Penguin.

FORSYTHE, B. (1988) Quo Vadis, Britannia? Black and White and Brown in Britain in the late 1980s, in *Perspectives 35, Ethnicity and Prejudice in White Highland Schools*, University of Exeter.

FOSTER, M. (1986) Monitoring the Schools: A Framework for Evaluation, *Multicultural Teaching*, **15**, 1.

FRANCIS, M. (1984) *Anti-Racist Teaching: General Principles in Challenging Racism*. London: ALTARF.

FULLER, M. (1983) *Conflict and Change in Education* (Unit E205, Block 6 Gender, Race and Class). Milton Keynes: Open University.

GAINE, C. (1987) *No Problem Here*. London: Heinemann.

GAINE, C. (1989) On Getting Equal Opportunities Policies and Keeping Them, in COLE, M. (ed), *Education for Equality*. London: Routledge and Kegan Paul.

GALLIERS, D. (1987) A Framework for Antiracist Training, *British Journal of Inservice Education*, **13**, 2.

GIBSON, M. (1976) Approaches to Multicultural Education in the United States: Some Concepts and Assumptions, *Anthropology and Education Quarterly*, 7, 4, 7–18.

GILL, B. (1989) Indicators and Institutional Evaluation, *Multicultural Teaching*, **8**, 1.

GLEDHILL, M. and HEFFERMAN, M. (1984) Racism Awareness Workshops for Teachers, *Education and Child Psychology*, **1**, 1.

GORDON, P. (1989) Just Another Asian Murder, *Guardian*, 20 July.

GRANT, C. A. and GRANT, G. W. (1985) Staff Development and Education that is Multicultural, *British Journal of Inservice Education*, **12**, 1.

GRANT, C. A. and SLEETER, C. E. (1985) The Literature on Multicultural Education: Review and Analysis, *Education Review*, **37**, 2.

GRANT, N. (1984) Education for a Multicultural Society, in CORNER, T. (ed.) *Multicultural Societies*. London: Croom Helm.

GREEN, A. (1982) In Defence of Anti-Racist Teaching, *Multicultural Teaching*, **1**, 2.

GREEN, P. A. (1985) Multi-Ethnic Teaching and the Pupils' Self-

Concepts (Annex B, The Committee of Enquiry into the Education of Children from Ethnic Minority Groups), *Education for All*. London: HMSO.

GRINTER, R. (1985) Bridging the Gulf: The Need for Anti-Racist Multicultural Education, *Multicultural Teaching*, **3**, 2.

GRINTER, R. (1989) Anti-racist Strategies in the National Curriculum, *Multicultural Teaching*, **7**, 3.

GRINTER, R. (1990) Transforming the National Curriculum: Developments in an antiracist campaign, *Multicultural Teaching*, **8**, 3.

GUNDARA, J. (1986) Education for a Multicultural Society, in GUNDARA, J.; JONES, C. and KIMBERLEY, K. (eds). *Racism, Diversity and Education*. London: Hodder and Stoughton.

GURMAH, A. (1984) The Politics RAT, *Critical Social Policy*, **61**, Winter.

GURMAH, A. (1987) Gatekeepers and Caretakers: Swann, Scarman and the Social Policy of Containment, in TROYNA, B. (ed.) *Racial Inequality in Education*. London: Tavistock.

HALL, S. (1980) Teaching Race, *Multi-Racial Education*, **9**, 3–13.

HALL, S. *et al*. (1978) *Policing the Crisis*. London: Macmillan.

HALSTEAD, M. (1988) *Education, Justice and Cultural Diversity: An Examination of the Honeyford Affair 1984–85*. London: Falmer Press.

HAMPSHIRE COUNTY COUNCIL (1988) *Education for a Multicultural Society*. Hampshire County Council Education Department.

HARRISON, S. (1986) Swann: The Implications for Schools, *Journal of Education Policy*, **1**, 2.

HATCHER, R. (1989) Anti-racist Education after the Act, *Multicultural Teaching*, **7**, 3.

HATCHER, R. and SHALLICE, J. (1983) The Politics of Anti-Racist Education, *Multicultural Education*, **12**, 1, 3–21.

HICKS, D. (1981) *Bias in Geography textbooks: Images of the Third World and Multi-Ethnic Education* (Working Paper No. 1). London: Centre for Multicultural Education, University of London.

HILL, D. (1989) *Out of his skin: The John Barnes Phenomenon* London: Faber and Faber.

HIRST, P. H. (1965) Liberal Education and The Nature of Knowledge, in PETERS, R. S. *The Philosophy of Education*. Oxford: Oxford University Press.

HIX. P. (forthcoming) *Educating for a Multicultural Society*. Wheatons.

HOME AFFAIRS COMMITTEE *Racial Disadvantage*, **1**, House of Commons

Paper 424, London: HMSO.

HONEYFORD, R. (1984) Education and Race: An Alternative View, *The Salisbury Review*, 6 (Winter) 16–19.

HONEYFORD, R. (1986) Anti-racist rhetoric, in PALMER, F. (ed.) *Anti-Racism: An Assault on Education and Value*. London: Sherwood Press.

HOPKINS, D. (1986) *Inservice Training and Educational Development: An International Survey*. London: Croom Helm.

HER MAJESTY'S STATIONERY OFFICE. (1981) *Racial Attitudes*. London: HMSO.

HER MAJESTY'S STATIONERY OFFICE (1986) *Bangladeshis in Britain*. London: HMSO.

HUGHES, L. Poor Little Black Fellow, in *The Ways of White Folks*. New York: Vintage.

ILEA (1984) *Race, Sex and Class*. London: County Hall.

INSTITUTE OF RACE RELATIONS Anti-racist not Multi-racial Education, IRR Statement to the Rampton Committee, *Race and Class*, **22**, 1.

JEFFCOATE, R. (1979) A Multi-cultural Curriculum Beyond the Orthodoxy, *Trends in Education*, **IV**, 8–12 and in *Positive Image*. London: Chameleon Books.

JEFFCOATE, R. (1984a) *Ethnic Minorities in Education*. London: Harper & Row.

JEFFCOATE, R. (1984b) Ideologies and Multi-cultural Education, in CRAFT, M. (ed.) *Education and Cultural Pluralism*. London: Falmer Press.

JOHNSON, J. W. (1950) *Autobiography of an Ex-Coloured Man*. New York: Hill and Wong.

JONES, C. (1986) Racism in Society and Schools, in GUNDARA, J.; JONES, C. and KIMBERLEY, K. (eds.) *Racism, Diversity and Education*. London: Hodder and Stoughton.

JONES, M. (1985) Education and Racism, *Journal of the Philosophy of Education*, **19**, 2.

KATZ, J. (1978) *White Awareness – A Handbook for Anti-Racism Training*. Oklahoma: University of Oklahoma Press.

KATZ, P. A. and ZALK, S. R. (1978) Modifications of Children's Racial Attitudes, *Development Psychology*, **14**, 447–61.

KELLY, E. and COHEN, T. (1988) *Racism in Schools: New Research Evidence*. Stoke-on-Trent: Trentham Books.

KERNER (1968) Report of the National Advisory Commission of Civil Disorders. New York: Bentom

KIMBERLEY, K. (1986) The School Curriculum, in GUNDARA, J.; JONES, C. and KIMBERLEY, K. (eds.). *Racism, Diversity and Education*. London: Hodder and Stoughton.

KIRP, D. *Doing Good by Doing Little*. London: University of California Press.

KLEIN, G. (1984) *Resources for Multicultural Education* Harlow: Longman.

KREJIL, J. and VELIMSKY, V. (1981) *Ethnic and Political Nations in Europe*. London: Croom Helm.

LABOV, W. (1969 and 1973) The Logic of Non-standard English, in KEDDIE, N. (ed.), *Tinker, Tailor ... The Myth of Cultural Deprivation*. Harmondsworth: Penguin.

LAWRENCE, J. and STEED, D. (1985) Predisposed to Violence, *Times Educational Supplement*, 7 June.

LEE, V., LEE, J. and PEARSON, M. (1987) Stories Children tell, in POLLARD, A. (ed.) *Children of Their Primary Schools: A New Perspective*. Lewes: Falmer Press.

LEICESTER, M. (1986) Education, Race and Resolution, *Journal of Moral Education*, **15**, 1.

LEICESTER, M. (1989) Deconstructing the Anti-Anti-racists Cognition, *Multicultural Teaching*, 7, 2.

LEWIS, R. (1980) *Anti-Racism – A Mania Exposed*. London: Quartet.

LITTLE, A. (1975). The Educational Achievement of Ethnic Minority Children in London Schools, in VERMA, G. K. and BAGLEY, C. (eds), *Race and Education Across Cultures*. London: Heinemann.

LITTLE, A. and WILLEY, R. (1981) *Multi-ethnic Education – The Way Forward*. London: Schools Council.

LITTLE, A. and WILLEY, R. (1983) *Studies in the Multi-ethnic Curriculum*. London: Schools Council.

LYNCH, J. (1983) *The Multi-cultural Curriculum*. London: Batsford.

LYNCH, J. (1984) Curriculum and Assessment, in CRAFT, M. (ed.) *Education and Cultural Pluralism*. London: Falmer Press.

LYNCH, J. (1986a) *Multicultural Education – Principles and Practice*. London: Routledge and Kegan Paul.

LYNCH, J. (1986b) Multicultural Education: Agenda for Change, in BANKS, J. A. and LYNCH, J. (eds.), *Multi-cultural Education in Western Societies*. London: Holt, Rinehart and Winston.

LYNCH, J. (1988) Prejudice Reduction and the Schools. London: Cassell.

LYSEIGHT-JONES (1989) A management of change perspective: Turning the whole school around in, COLE, M. (ed.) *Education for Equality*. London: Routledge and Kegan Paul.

MACDONALD, I. *et al.* (1989) *Murder in the Playground*. London: Longseight.

MAITLAND, S. (1989) *Multicultural Inset, A Practical Handbook for Teachers*. Stoke on Trent: Trentham Books.

MANCHESTER LEA (1980) *Education for a Multicultural Society*. Manchester.

MASSEY, I. (1987) Hampshire Happening, *Multicultural Teaching*, **5**, 2.

MILES, R. (1982) *Racism and Migrant Labour*. London: Routledge and Kegan Paul.

MILES, R. (1984) Racialization, in CASHMORE, E.E (ed.), *Dictionary of Race and Ethnic Relations*. London: Routledge and Kegan Paul.

MILES, R. (1988) *Racism*. London: Routledge and Kegan Paul.

MILNER, D. (1983) *Children and Race Ten Years On*. London: Ward Lock.

MINHAS, R. (1988) The Politics Behind the National Curriculum, *Multicultural Teaching*, **6**, 2.

MINHAS, R. (1989) LMS Pandora's Box or a Panacea for Improving the Quality of State Education, *Multicultural Teaching*, **8**, 1.

MITCHELL, P. *et al.* (1984) Developing a Whole-School Anti-racist Policy in M. STRAKER-WELDES (ed.) *Education for a Multicultural Society*. London: Bell and Hyman.

MODGIL, S. *et al.* (1986) *Multicultural Education: The Interminable Debate*. London: Falmer Press.

MOULD, W. (1986) No Rainbow coalition on Tyneside, *Multi-cultural Teaching*, **IV**, 3.

MULLARD, C. (1981) *Racism, Society and Schools*. London: University of London.

MYRDAL, G. (1944) *The American Dilemma, The Negro Problem and Modern Democracies*. New York: Harper and Row.

NATIONAL CURRICULUM COUNCIL (1988) *Welcome to the NCC*. London.

NATIONAL CURRICULUM COUNCIL (1989) *The National Curriculum and Whole Curriculum Planning*, (Circular 6). London.

NATIONAL CURRICULUM COUNCIL (1990) *The Whole Curriculum*. London.

NIXON, J. (1985) *A Teacher's Guide to Multicultural Education*. London: Blackwell.

NIXON, J. and WATTS, M. (1989) *Whole School Approaches to Multicultural Education*. Basingstoke: Macmillan.

NORTH WESTMINSTER COMMUNITY SCHOOL (1982) *Towards a Multi-*

cultural Philosophy. London.

O'KEEFE, D. (ed.) (1986) *The Wayward Curriculum, A Cause for Parents' Concern*. London: Social Affairs Unit.

OLDMAN, D. (1987) Plain speaking and pseudo-Science: the New Right Attack on Anti-racism in, TROYNA, B. (ed.) *Racial Equality in Education*. London: Tavistock.

PAGE and THOMAS (1984) *Multicultural Education and the All-White School*. University of Nottingham, Education Department.

PALMER, F. (ed.) (1986) *Anti-racism: An Assault on Education and Value*. London: Sherwood Press.

PAREKH, B. (1986) the Concept of Multicultural Education, in MODGIL, S. *et al.* (eds), *Multicultural Education: The Interminable Debate*. London: Falmer Press.

PAREKH, B. (1988) *Better to light a candle ... more multicultural education* (Perspectives 39). University of Exeter.

PAREKH, B. (1989) The Hermeneutics of the Swann Report, in VERMA G.K. (ed) and PEARCE, S. *Education for All: A Landmark in Pluralism*. London: Falmer Press.

PEARCE, S. (1986) Swann and the Spirit of the Age, in PALMER, F. (ed.) *Anti-racism: An Assault on Education and Value*. London: Sherwood Press.

PEPPARD, N. (1983) RAT *New Community*, **XI**, 1 & 2, Winter.

PETERS, R. S. (1965) *Ethnics and Education*. London: George Allen and Unwin.

POLLACK, M. (1972) A Suggested Black Studies Syllabus, *Teachers Against Racism*, 7, 10–11.

QUINTON KYNASTON SCHOOL (1980) *Policy on Racist Behaviour: A Statement for the Staff Handbook*. Marlborough Hill, London.

REEVES, F. (1983) *British Racial Discourse: A Study of British Political Discourse About Race and Race Related Matters*. Cambridge: Cambridge University Press.

RICH, P. (1989) Review of Miles R. 'Racism', *New Community*, **16**, 1.

RICHARDS, C. (1986) Anti-racist Initiatives, **Screen**, 77, 5.

RIZVI, F. (1989) Pedling a culture of irrationalities: A Critique of Anti-Racism – A Mania Exposed, *Multicultural Teaching*, 7, 2.

REX, J. (1986) Equality of Opportunity and the Ethnic Minority child in British Schools, in MODGIL, S. *et al.* (eds), *Multicultural Education: The Interminable Debate*. London: Falmer Press.

REX, J. (1986) *Education for Some*. Stoke on Trent: Trentham Books.

REX, J. (1989) Equality of Opportunity, Multiculturalism, Anti-Racism and Education for All, in VERMA G. K. (ed.) *Education for All*. London: Falmer Press.

ROBERTS, A. and MASSEY, I. (forthcoming) School Based Management of Change, in FYFE, A. and FIGUEROA, P. (eds) *Education for Cultural Diversity*. Basingstoke: Macmillan.

ROSE, D. (1987) Article in the *Guardian*, 6 February, p.11.

ROSE, E. J. B. *et al* (1969) Colour and Citizenship. Institute of Race Relations. London: Oxford University Press.

ROSE, S., LETWONTIN, R. C. and KAMLIN, L. J. (1984) *Not in our Genes*. Harmondsworth: Penguin.

RUSHDIE, S. (1982) The New Empire in Britain, *New Society*, 9 December.

SACHS, J. (1986) Putting Culture Back into Multicultural Education, *New Community*, **13**, 2.

SAID, A. A. and STIMMONS, L. R. (eds) (1976) *Ethnicity in an International Context*. New Brunswick: Transaction Books.

SCHOOLS COUNCIL (1967) *English for the Children of Immigrants* (Working Paper No. 13). London: HMSO.

SCRUTON, R. (1986) The Myth of Cultural Relation, in O'KEEFE, D. (ed.) *Anti-racism: An Assault on Education and Value*. London: Sherwood Press.

SHALLICE, J. (1983) Formulating an Anti-racist Policy at the Skinners School, *Multi-ethnic Education Review*, **2**, 2.

SIVANANDAN, A. (1984) RAT the Degradation of the Black Struggle, *Race and Class* **26**, 4.

SLAVIN R.E. (1983) *Cooperative Learning*. London: Methuen.

SMITH, D. J. (1977) *Racial Disadvantage in Britain*. Harmondsworth: Penguin.

SMITH, D. J. and GRAY, J. (1983) *Police and People in London: The Police in Action*. London: Policy Studies Institute.

SMITH, D. J. and TOMLINSON, S. (1989) *The School Effect*. London: Policy Studies Institute.

SMITH, J. (1989) Anti-Racist practice after the Act: What are the ways forward? *Multicultural Teaching*, **7**, 3.

SPEARS, A. K. (1978) Institutional Racism and the Education of Blacks, *Anthropology and Education Quarterly*, **9**, 2, 127–36.

STONE, M. (1981) *The Education of the Black Child in Britain: The Myth of Multi-racial Education*. London: Fontana.

STROHNACH, I. and AKHTAR, S. (1986) They call me Blacky, *Times Educational Supplement*, September.

TAYLOR, B. (1986) Anti-racist Education in Non-contact Areas: The Need for a Gentler Approach, *New Community*, **13**, 2, Autumn.

THIRD WORLD SCIENCE PROJECT (1986). Bangor, University of North Wales, School of Education.

TIERNEY, J. (ed.) (1982) *Race. Migration and Schooling*. London: Holt International.

TOMLINSON, S. (1979). Decision Making in Special Education (ESNM) with some reference to children and immigrant parentage (Unpublished Phd Thesis). University of Warwick.

TOMLINSON, S. (1980) The Educational Performance of Ethnic Minority Children, *New Community,* **8,** 3, Winter.

TOMLINSON, S. (1982) *Educational Subnormality: A Study in Decision-Making.* London: Routledge and Kegan Paul.

TOMLINSON, S. (1986) Ethnicity and Educational Achievement, in MODGIL, S. *et al.* (eds) *Multicultural Education: The Intermediate Debate.* London: Falmer Press.

TOMLINSON, S. (1989) The Origins of an Ethnocentric Curriculum, in VERMA, G. K. (ed.) *Education for All. A Landmark in Pluralism.* London: Falmer Press.

TOMLINSON, S. AND COULSON, P. (1988) *A Descriptive Analysis of a Sample of Projects Funded by Educational Support Grants in Mainly White Areas.* University of Lancaster.

TROYNA, B. AND BALL, W. (1985) *Views from the Chalk Face: School Responses to an LEA's Policy on Multicultural Education.* Centre for Research in Ethnic Relations, University of Warwick.

TROYNA, B. AND WILLIAMS, J. (1986) *Racism, Education and the State.* London: Croom Helm.

TROYNA, B. AND SELMAN, L. (1989) Surviving in the 'Survivalist Culture', Anti-racist strategies in the new ERA, *Journal of Further and Higher Education,* **13**, 2.

TWITCHIN, J. AND DEMUTH, C. *Multicultural Education: Views from the Classroom.* London: BBC.

VERMA, G.K. (ed.) (1989) *Education for All. A Landmark in Pluralism.* London: Falmer Press.

WALVIN, J. (1973) *Black and White: The Negro in British Society 1555-1945.* London: Allen Lane.

WALVIN, J. (1986) *Football and the Decline of Britain.* Basingstoke: Macmillan.

WAUGH, A. (1985) Time for the animals of Merseyside to be put in uniform, *The Spectator,* June, p.8.

WILLEY, R. (1984) *Race, Equality and Schools.* London: Methuen.

WRIGHT, C. (1985) The Influence of School Processes on the Educational Opportunities of Children of West Indian Origin, *Multicultural Teaching,* 4, 1, 11-22.

YATES, P.D. (1986) Figure and Section: Ethnography and Education in the Multi-cultural State, in MODGIL, S. *et al.* (eds), *Multicultural Education: The Interminable Debate.* London: Falmer Press.

ZEC, P. (1980) Multicultural Education: What Kind of Relativism is Possible?, *Journal of Philosophy of Education,* 14, 1.

Index

achievement   59–61, 67–8
access to information on multicultural
    education resources   81
anti-racism   3, 4, 15–17, 18, 23, 35, 44,
    97, 115, 125
anti-racist multicultural education   6,
    17–21, 28, 29, 42, 52, 53, 55, 60, 70,
    72, 80, 81, 87, 90, 91, 96, 100, 102,
    103, 118, 154
anti-semitism   1, 63
art   74, 93, 146
assimilation   9–11, 57, 63, 103

Berkshire LEA   16, 24
bilingualism   75
biology   145
Burnage Report (MacDonald
    Inquiry)   125

Canada   170
collaborative learning   97
compensation   11–12
condensation symbols   45
cross-curricular themes   86, 93, 98
culture   48, 49, 57, 63, 68
    inferior/superior   10, 61–2, 64
    pluralism   12–15, 46–7, 50–2, 53, 55,
        63, 105

design and technology   83–4
demographic changes   68–70, 90
discrimination   2, 12, 15, 16, 65
drama   74, 93, 146

Education Reform Act (ERA)   6, 27, 30,
    81, 89, 94, 154
education support grants   21, 27, 28, 29
English   22, 74, 82–3, 145
ESN schools   37, 38
equality of opportunity   29, 68, 57
ethnic monitoring   91, 93
ethnic revitalisation   71–2

evaluation   115, 137–41, 144–8, 153,
    155, 156

Fascism, genteel   42, 80
football
    hooliganism   2
    racial abuse   3–4
Frogmore Community School   127–56,
    157–66

geography   74, 146
good practice   73, 100, 103, 104, 129

history   74, 84, 146
home economics   22, 146

ILEA   16, 23, 24, 142
immigration
    figures   8
    laws   16, 37
    pupil views   78–9
    trends   1, 63, 64
indoctrination   35, 54, 67
INSET   86, 92, 105, 106, 117–20,
    141–3, 154
integration   11–12
intercultural education   29

laissez-faire   9
LMS   90, 91, 92, 116, 154
managing change   103–26
managing strategies   119, 132
maths   74, 145
modern languages   74, 145
mono-cultural curriculum   63, 74,
    75–6, 95–6, 100
multicultural education   3, 13, 18, 22,
    23, 29, 43, 47, 48, 51, 55, 57, 63, 73,
    100
multicultural guidelines   47, 49, 50, 51,
    86
music   74, 93, 147

National Curriculum 6, 29, 30, 81, 92, 94, 96, 98, 154
'New Right' 54, 58

parents 126, 150–3
pedagogy 96
peer tutoring 98
people of colour 69
performance indicators 91
PE (dance) 146
physics 146
policies
  LEA 14, 16, 22, 23, 24, 35, 39, 43–6, 56, 68, 104, 128
  school 3, 21, 22, 24, 26, 41
PSE 97, 147

race 20, 31, 156
racial
  abuse 2, 27, 65, 89, 136
  incidents 26, 135, 136, 147
  violence 2, 15–16, 60, 65
Racial Awareness Training (RAT) 108, 118–26, 129

racialisation 16, 43
racism 3, 4, 5, 15, 21, 29, 31–5, 57, 68, 72, 109, 111, 113
  development 63–4
  institutional 5, 29, 36–43, 71, 128
  pupil views 65–6, 76, 79–80, 147–9

science 74, 83
school exchanges 98–100
social studies 74, 147
staff development 27, 101–2, 105–8, 120–2, 156
Swann Report 3, 19, 20, 21, 26, 27, 28, 57, 58, 59, 68, 79–80, 115

teacher stereotyping 24, 27, 38, 39, 58–9

'whiteness' 110
whole curriculum 85–6
whole school policies 112, 118, 128, 148, 154
working parties 112, 122–4, 127–32, 154